# PHILEMON

## "THE POWER OF LOVE AND RECONCILIATION"

V. SOURAB

# Contents

# Dedication

*To all those seeking reconciliation and the transformative power of love, dedicated to the spirit of forgiveness and the hope of restoration, for anyone who believes in the power of love to heal and unite.*

*This book is dedicated to the enduring message of Philemon: that love and reconciliation can bridge any divide. May its wisdom inspire us all to extend grace and embrace forgiveness.*

*Dedicated to the timeless truth in the letter to Philemon, a testament to the transformative power of Christ's love.*

*This work is dedicated to the enduring message of Philemon, a call to embrace reconciliation and extend grace as Christ has extended it to us and the power of the Gospel, as exemplified in Philemon, which demonstrates that love can overcome any barrier.*

*To those who have shown me the power of love and reconciliation in their lives, and to all who strive to embody these virtues.*

*In loving memory of those who taught me the importance of forgiveness, and in hopeful anticipation of a world where reconciliation prevails. Dedicated To my **Sunday School Teacher Mrs. M. Sathyavathi Garu (Late), ExSuperintendent of Sunday School, The Lone Star Telugu Baptist Church – 1ˢᵗ Service Nellore**, whose unwavering support and love have made this journey possible, who inspired me to delve deeper into the message of Philemon and share its wisdom with the world.*

*And finally, to all those who have struggled with forgiveness, may this book offer hope and encouragement. For the mending of broken bridges, the healing of wounded hearts, and the enduring power of love to reconcile.*

*- V. Sourab*

# Foreword

*In an age where the threads of our shared humanity often seem frayed and discord runs rampant, the timeless message of Philemon emerges as a beacon of hope and reconciliation.* **"Philemon: The Power of Love and Reconciliation"** *seeks to breathe life into an ancient letter, unveiling its enduring relevance and transformative power for our contemporary world.*

*The story of Philemon is a profound testament to the radical nature of love and the boundless possibilities of reconciliation. It is an invitation to transcend barriers, heal wounds, and foster relationships rooted in compassion and understanding. As you journey through these pages, you will discover that the lessons embedded in Philemon's narrative are not merely historical artefacts but living principles that can reshape our lives and communities.*

*This book is a labour of love, born from a deep desire to explore the intersections of faith, forgiveness, and human connection. It challenges us to reflect on our own lives and the ways we can embody the spirit of Philemon in our interactions with others. Through the lens of love and reconciliation, we are called to envision a world where justice and mercy walk hand in hand.*

*I hope that* **"Philemon: The Power of Love and Reconciliation"** *will inspire you to embrace the transformative potential of these values. May it empower you to be an agent of change, cultivating harmony and understanding in a world that so desperately needs it. Let us embark on this journey together, with open hearts and minds, ready to be transformed by the profound wisdom of Philemon.*

*- V. Sourab*

# Preface

*The journey of writing **"Philemon: The Power of Love and Reconciliation"** has been both a deeply personal and profoundly enlightening experience. The epistle of Philemon, though brief, offers a rich tapestry of themes that resonate with the essence of human relationships—love, forgiveness, and the pursuit of reconciliation.*

*In a world often marked by division and discord, the message of Philemon serves as a timeless reminder of the transformative power of love and the potential for reconciliation. It compels us to look beyond our differences and seek common ground, fostering a spirit of unity and understanding. This book explores these enduring values, inviting readers to reflect on their own lives and how they can embody the principles of Philemon.*

*Throughout this work, I have endeavoured to delve into the historical, cultural, and theological contexts of the epistle, unveiling its relevance for contemporary readers. I hope that by engaging with the narrative of Philemon, readers will find inspiration and encouragement to pursue reconciliation in their relationships and communities.*

*Writing this book has been a labour of love, fuelled by a desire to share the profound wisdom of Philemon with a wider audience. It is my sincerest hope that **"Philemon: The Power of Love and Reconciliation"** will not only illuminate the timeless truths of the epistle but also spark a movement of love and reconciliation in our world today.*

*I invite you to join me on this journey, as we explore the depths of Philemon's message and discover the boundless possibilities of love and reconciliation.*

*- V. Sourab*

# Acknowledgements

*Completing **"Philemon: The Power of Love and Reconciliation"** would not have been possible without many individuals' unwavering support, encouragement, and inspiration.*

*First and foremost, I am profoundly grateful to my family for their love, patience, and belief in me throughout this journey, especially to **my Grandfather Mr. Chadalawada Prabhakara Rao, Retired Head Master,** whose support has been my anchor, and whose encouragement has fuelled my passion for writing.*

*I extend my heartfelt thanks to **Rev. Kancharla Prabhudas, Pastor, The Lone Star Telugu Baptist Church – 1st service Nellore,** who has been my sounding board, providing invaluable feedback and insights that have shaped the direction of this book. Your thoughtful contributions and candid discussions have enriched the content in ways I could not have imagined.*

*Lastly, I wish to thank the readers who have embarked on this journey with me. Your curiosity and openness to the message of Philemon inspire me to continue exploring the depths of love and reconciliation.*

*To all those who have been part of this endeavour, I am eternally grateful. This book is a testament to your support and the power of community.*

*- V. Sourab*

# Prologue

*In the bustling streets of ancient Colossae, amid the clamour of daily life and the intricate web of social hierarchies, a remarkable story unfolds. It is a story that transcends the boundaries of time and place, echoing through the ages with a message of love, forgiveness, and reconciliation.*

*At the heart of this narrative lies a simple yet profound letter, penned by the Apostle Paul to a fellow believer, Philemon. This epistle, though brief, captures the essence of a radical and transformative love that challenges the status quo and seeks to restore broken relationships. It is a testament to the power of grace and the boundless potential for healing and unity.*

*As you embark on this journey through **"Philemon: The Power of Love and Reconciliation,"** you will be transported to a world where the values of compassion and forgiveness are brought to life in vivid detail. The characters within these pages are not mere figures of antiquity but living, breathing individuals whose struggles and triumphs mirror our own.*

*This book is an invitation to delve into the depths of Philemon's message, to uncover the layers of meaning that speak to the human condition and the complexities of our relationships. It is a call to embrace the transformative power of love and to seek reconciliation in our own lives and communities.*

*Let the timeless wisdom of Philemon guide you as we journey together through a narrative that has the potential to change hearts and minds. May this story inspire you to look beyond the surface, to see the humanity in others, and to cultivate a spirit of love and reconciliation in all that you do.*

*- **V. Sourab***

# CHAPTER ONE

# INTRODUCTION

## A. OVERVIEW

The Book of Philemon Is a Deeply Personal and Profound Letter Written by The Apostle Paul. Despite Its Brevity (Just 25 Verses), The Epistle Holds Enduring Importance for Its Reflection on Christian Relationships and The Transformative Power of Faith in Jesus Christ. Through This Letter, Paul Masterfully Addresses Themes of Forgiveness, Reconciliation, And Brotherly Love in A Specific Situation: The Relationship Between a Christian Slave Owner, Philemon, And His Runaway Slave, Onesimus.

### 1. Philemon As a Unique Epistle

The Letter to Philemon Stands Out Among Paul's Writings Because It Is Neither a Doctrinal Dissertation nor An Address to A Church Body. Instead, It Is a Private Correspondence—An Appeal from Paul to His Friend and Fellow Worker in Christ, Philemon. While The Letter Primarily Deals with A Personal Matter, Its Message Transcends the Individual Situation to Convey Principles of Christian Ethics and Community.

Unlike Many of Paul's Other Epistles, Such as Romans or Galatians, Which Emphasize Theological Arguments, Philemon Is Intensely Relational. The Letter Provides a Vivid Example of How Christian Teachings Can Be Applied to Social and Interpersonal

Issues. In This Sense, It Mirrors the Practical Application of Christ's Teachings Found in Passages Like Matthew 5:9 ("Blessed Are the Peacemakers") And Matthew 18:21-22 (Jesus' Teaching on Forgiveness).

## 2. Setting And Context

Paul wrote this letter during his imprisonment, which he traditionally believed to be in Rome, around A.D. 60-62. During This Time, Paul Was Heavily Engaged in Guiding the Early Christian Communities Through Letters and Teachings. Philemon, The Recipient of This Letter, Was A Wealthy Christian in Colossae and A Leader in The Local Church (Philemon 1:1-2). Onesimus, His Slave, Had Fled and Later Encountered Paul, Through Whom He Became a Christian Believer (Philemon 1:10-11).

Runaway Slaves in The Roman Empire Faced Severe Consequences, Including Punishment or Death. However, Paul's Intercession on Behalf of Onesimus Demonstrates a Radical Reimagining of Social Relationships Through the Lens of The Gospel. Paul does not merely ask for Onesimus' Pardon but urges Philemon to accept Him as a brother in Christ who is equal in faith and love (Philemon 1:16).

This Appeal Aligns with Paul's Broader Teachings on Equality in Christ, As Seen in Galatians 3:28: "There Is Neither Jew nor Gentile, Neither Slave nor Free, Nor Is There Male and Female, For You Are All One in Christ Jesus." Through This Letter, Paul Illustrates How Faith in Jesus Transforms Human Relationships, Transcending Societal Norms and Hierarchies.

## 3. Reconciliation Through Christ

At Its Heart, The Book of Philemon Is About Reconciliation. Paul Serves as A Mediator Between Philemon and Onesimus, Advocating for Restoration and Unity. This Role Mirrors the 'Work of Christ, Who Reconciles Humanity to God (2 Corinthians 5:18-19). Paul's

Willingness to Take on Onesimus' Debts (Philemon 1:18-19) Exemplifies the Sacrificial Love of Jesus, Who Took on The Sins of Humanity (Romans 5:8).

The Letter Demonstrates That Reconciliation Is Not Merely a Personal or Social Matter but A Spiritual One. By Urging Philemon To Forgive and Embrace Onesimus, Paul Underscores the Transformative Power of The Gospel to Heal Relationships and Create a New Community in Christ.

## 4. A Model of Christian Love

Paul's Approach in The Letter Models Christian Love in Action. He Addresses Philemon with Respect and Affection, Expressing Gratitude for His Faith and Love Toward the Saints (Philemon 1:4-7). Paul's Tone Is Not Commanding but Persuasive, Appealing to Philemon's Conscience and Faith. This Approach Reflects the Principle Found in John 13:34-35, Where Jesus Commands His Disciples to Love One Another As He Has Loved Them.

Moreover, Paul's Letter Serves as A Reminder That Christian Love Is Not Abstract but Practical and Relational. It Involves Forgiveness, Humility, And Seeing Others Through the Eyes of Christ. As Paul Writes in Colossians 3:13-14, Believers Are Called To "Bear With Each Other And Forgive One Another" And to Put on Love, which Binds Everything Together in Perfect Harmony.

## 5. A Living Testimony

The Book of Philemon Also Serves as A Living Testimony to The Early Christian Community's Ideals. By Addressing Philemon, Apphia, Archippus, And the Church Meeting In Their Home (Philemon 1:1-2), Paul Emphasizes The Communal Nature Of Faith. The Reconciliation Between Philemon And Onesimus Would Not Only Impact Their Relationship But Also Serve As A Powerful Witness To The Transformative Power Of The Gospel Within The Church.

In This Way, Philemon Parallels The Teachings Of Jesus In The Sermon On The Mount, Particularly The Call To Be Peacemakers (Matthew 5:9) And To Love One's Enemies (Matthew 5:44). It Also Resonates With Paul's Teachings In Ephesians 4:1-3, Where He Urges Believers To Live In A Manner Worthy Of Their Calling, Marked By Humility, Gentleness, And Patience.

# B. CONTEXT OF ITS WRITING

## 1. Historical And Cultural Setting

The Letter To Philemon Was Written By The Apostle Paul During One Of His Imprisonments, Traditionally Believed To Be In Rome Around A.D. 60-62 (Philemon 1:9, 13). At This Time, The Roman Empire Was A Dominant Power, With Slavery Being A Pervasive And Accepted Institution. Historians Estimate That Slaves Comprised A Significant Portion Of The Population, And Their Status Was Often One Of Servitude And Subjugation. Onesimus, The Central Figure In The Letter Apart From Paul And Philemon, Was One Such Slave Who Had Run Away From His Master, Philemon.

Runaway Slaves Faced Severe Punishments Under Roman Law, Ranging From Beatings To Execution. However, When Onesimus Encountered Paul During His Flight, His Life Took A Transformational Turn. Under Paul's Mentorship, Onesimus Became A Follower Of Christ And, Consequently, A "New Creation" (2 Corinthians 5:17). Paul's Letter To Philemon Reflects His Deep Commitment To Reconciliation And The Radical Redefinition Of Relationships Within The Christian Faith.

The Cultural Context Is Crucial To Understanding The Radical Nature Of Paul's Appeal. Slavery In The Roman World Was Not Merely An Economic System But A Deeply Ingrained Social Hierarchy. By Advocating For Onesimus' Acceptance As A "Beloved Brother" (Philemon 1:16), Paul Challenged These Societal Norms With The Gospel's Transformative Power. This Aligns With Paul's Teaching In Galatians 3:28, Where He Declares That In Christ, "There Is Neither Slave Nor Free."

## 2. Paul's Imprisonment And Ministry

Paul's Imprisonment Did Not Deter His Missionary Work. While Confined, He Wrote Several Epistles, Often Referred To As The "Prison Epistles," Which Include Ephesians, Philippians, Colossians, And Philemon. These Letters Were Vital In Guiding And Strengthening The Early Christian Communities.

In Colossians 4:7-9, We Find A Direct Connection To Onesimus, Who Is Mentioned As A "Faithful And Beloved Brother." This Indicates That The Letter To Philemon Was Likely Written Around The Same Time As The Letter To The Colossians. Both Epistles Were Delivered By Tychicus And Onesimus, Further Demonstrating Their Intertwined Narratives.

Paul's Situation In Prison Also Highlights His Role As A Spiritual Father And Mediator. Despite His Physical Confinement, Paul Continued To Advocate For Justice, Reconciliation, And The Spread Of The Gospel. His Willingness To Mediate Between Philemon And Onesimus Mirrors The Redemptive Work Of Christ, Who Reconciled Humanity To God (Romans 5:10; 2 Corinthians 5:18-19).

## 3. *The Relationship Between Paul, Philemon, And Onesimus*

Paul's Relationship With Philemon Is Evident In The Opening Verses Of The Letter, Where Paul Addresses Him As A "Beloved Friend And Fellow Worker" (Philemon 1:1). This Greeting Sets A Tone Of Mutual Respect And Affection, Which Underpins Paul's Appeal On Behalf Of Onesimus.

Philemon Was A Christian Leader In Colossae, Likely Hosting A Church In His Home (Philemon 1:2). This Reflects The Early Christian Practice Of Meeting In Private Homes, As Seen In Other Parts Of The New Testament (Acts 2:46; Romans 16:5). Paul's Acknowledgment Of Philemon's Faith And Love (Philemon 1:4-7) Highlights His Reputation Within The Christian Community.

Onesimus, Whose Name Means "Useful," Had Previously Been "Useless" To Philemon, Likely Due To His Status As A Runaway

Slave (Philemon 1:11). However, His Conversion To Christianity Through Paul Transformed His Identity And Purpose. In Christ, Onesimus Became More Than A Servant; He Became A Brother And Fellow Believer. This Transformation Echoes The Message Of 1 Corinthians 12:13, Which Emphasizes The Unity Of All Believers In The Body Of Christ.

## 4. Paul's Appeal For Reconciliation

The Letter To Philemon Serves As A Case Study In Christian Reconciliation. Paul Appeals To Philemon Not Based On Authority But Out Of Love (Philemon 1:8-9). This approach reflects the humility and gentleness that Paul advocates in Ephesians 4:1-3, which urges believers to live in a manner worthy of their calling.

Paul's Willingness To Assume Onesimus' Debt (Philemon 1:18-19) Is A Powerful Demonstration Of Christ-Like Mediation. By Taking On Onesimus' Burden, Paul Mirrors The Sacrificial Love Of Jesus, Who Bore The Sins Of Humanity (Isaiah 53:4-6; 1 Peter 2:24). This Act Also Serves As A Practical Example Of Bearing One Another's Burdens, As Instructed In Galatians 6:2.

Moreover, Paul's Request For Philemon To Welcome Onesimus As He Would Welcome Paul Himself (Philemon 1:17) Underscores The Radical Equality And Unity Found In Christ. This Aligns With The Teaching In Matthew 25:40, Where Jesus Emphasizes That Acts Of Love And Kindness Toward Others Are Ultimately Acts Done Unto Him.

## 5. The Broader Implications Of The Letter

While The Letter To Philemon Addresses A Specific Situation, Its Implications Extend Far Beyond The Personal Relationship Between Philemon And Onesimus. Paul's Appeal Challenges The Social Norms Of His Time, Offering A Vision Of A Christian Community Where Love, Forgiveness, And Equality Prevail.

This Vision Is Not Limited To The First-Century Roman World But Remains Relevant For Believers Today. The Letter Invites Readers To Reflect On Their Relationships And Consider How The Gospel Can Bring About Reconciliation And Transformation. It Also Serves As A Reminder Of The Cost Of Discipleship And The Call To Live Out Christ's Love In Practical And Tangible Ways.

# C. KEY THEMES AND PURPOSE OF THE LETTER.

## *KEY THEMES*

### 1. *Forgiveness And Reconciliation*

At The Heart Of The Book Of Philemon Is The Theme Of Forgiveness And Reconciliation. Paul Appeals To Philemon To Forgive His Runaway Slave, Onesimus, And To Welcome Him Back Not As A Servant But As A Brother In Christ (Philemon 1:16-17). This Reflects The Transformative Power Of The Gospel, Which Calls Believers To Mend Broken Relationships And Extend Forgiveness, Mirroring God's Forgiveness Of Humanity.
**Connecting Verses:**

- Matthew 6:14-15: Jesus Emphasizes The Necessity Of Forgiving Others, Stating That Forgiveness From God Is Contingent Upon Our Forgiveness Toward Others.
- 2 Corinthians 5:18-19: Paul Explains That God Reconciled Us To Himself Through Christ And Gave Us The Ministry Of Reconciliation, A Theme Exemplified In This Epistle.
- Colossians 3:13: Paul Urges Believers To Forgive One Another Just As The Lord Has Forgiven Them, Reinforcing The Principle Of Grace And Mercy In Relationships.

Through This Act Of Reconciliation, Paul Invites Philemon To Rise Above Societal Expectations And Live Out The Radical Equality And Love Demanded By Faith In Jesus. Forgiveness Is Not Merely An Option But An Expression Of Christ's Transformative Work In Believers' Lives.

## 2. *Christian Love In Action*

The Letter Showcases Love As A Central Tenet Of Christian Living. Paul Demonstrates Love Not Only In His Words To Philemon But Also Through His Actions As A Mediator For Onesimus. His Plea Is Rooted in Love Rather Than Authority, As He Writes, "I Appeal to You based on Love" (Philemon 1:9).

Paul's Acknowledgment of Philemon's Love and Faith (Philemon 1:4-7) Establishes the Foundation Upon Which He Makes His Appeal. This Shows How Christian Love Is Not Passive but Active, Guiding Believers to Act in Kindness, Humility, And Generosity.

**Connecting Verses:**

- John 13:34-35: Jesus Commands His Disciples to Love One Another As He Has Loved Them, Identifying Love as The Defining Mark of His Followers.
- 1 Corinthians 13:4-7: Paul's Famous Description of Love Provides a Blueprint for The Selfless and Sacrificial Love That He Demonstrates in His Advocacy for Onesimus.
- Galatians 5:14: "For the Entire Law Is Fulfilled in Keeping This One Command: 'Love Your Neighbor as Yourself.'"

By Writing This Letter, Paul Challenges Philemon to Extend This Kind of Love to Onesimus, Breaking Down Social Barriers and Living Out the Transformative Power of The Gospel.

## 3. *Equality And Brotherhood in Christ*

Another Powerful Theme in Philemon Is the Equality of All Believers in Christ. Onesimus, A Slave, Is No Longer to Be Regarded as Property but As a Beloved Brother in The Lord (Philemon 1:16). This Reflects the Radical Redefinition of Relationships Brought About by Faith in Jesus, Where Societal Hierarchies Are Dissolved, And All Are United in The Body of Christ.

**Connecting Verses:**

- Galatians 3:28: Paul Declares, "There Is Neither Jew nor Gentile, Neither Slave nor Free, Nor Is There Male and Female, For You Are All One in Christ Jesus."
- Ephesians 2:14-15: Paul Highlights How Christ Has Broken Down the Dividing Wall of Hostility, Creating Unity and Peace Among Believers.
- 1 Corinthians 12:13: "For We Were All Baptized by One Spirit So As To Form One Body—Whether Jews Or Gentiles, Slave Or Free."

This Theme Of Equality Challenges The Societal Norms Of The Roman Empire, Where Slavery Was An Accepted Institution. Paul's Appeal Exemplifies The Transformative Power Of The Gospel To Create A New Community In Which All Are Equal Before God.

## 4. Paul As A Christ-Like Mediator

Paul's Role In The Letter Mirrors The Work Of Christ As A Mediator. He Intercedes On Behalf Of Onesimus, Offering To Take On Any Debt Or Wrong Onesimus Owes To Philemon (Philemon 1:18-19). This Act Of Selflessness Reflects The Heart Of The Gospel, Where Christ Takes On The Sins Of Humanity To Reconcile Us To God (Romans 5:8; 2 Corinthians 5:21).

**Connecting Verses:**

- 1 Timothy 2:5: Paul Describes Jesus As The Mediator Between God And Humanity, A Role Paul Emulates In His Advocacy For Onesimus.
- Isaiah 53:4-6: This Old Testament Passage Foreshadows Christ's Sacrificial Work, Bearing The Sins Of Others, As Paul Figuratively Does For Onesimus.
- John 15:13: "Greater Love Has No One Than This: To Lay Down One's Life For One's Friends."

Paul's Willingness To Bear Onesimus' Burden Showcases The Depth Of His Commitment To Christ's Teachings And Serves As An Example For Believers To Follow In Their Relationships.

## 5. *The Transformative Power Of The Gospel*

The Letter To Philemon Underscores The Gospel's Ability To Transform Individuals And Communities. Onesimus, Once A Runaway Slave, Is Now Described As A "Faithful And Beloved Brother" (Colossians 4:9), Highlighting The Dramatic Change Brought About By His Encounter With Christ.

This Transformation Extends Beyond Onesimus To Philemon And The Wider Christian Community, Challenging Them To Embody The Gospel's Values In Their Daily Lives. The Letter Calls Believers To Reimagine Their Relationships In Light Of Christ's Redemptive Work.

**Connecting Verses:**

- 2 Corinthians 5:17: "Therefore, If Anyone Is In Christ, The New Creation Has Come: The Old Has Gone, The New Is Here!"
- Romans 12:2: Paul Urges Believers To Be Transformed By The Renewing Of Their Minds, Reflecting The Spiritual Renewal Seen In Onesimus.
- Philippians 1:6: Paul's Confidence That God Will Complete The Good Work He Began In Believers Resonates With The Transformation Evident In Onesimus' Life.

Through The Story Of Onesimus, Paul Illustrates How The Gospel Redefines Identity, Purpose, And Relationships, Creating A Community Marked By Love, Forgiveness, And Equality.

# *PURPOSE OF THE LETTER*

The Letter To Philemon Serves Multiple Purposes, Both Immediate And Enduring. On The Surface, It Addresses A Specific Personal Matter Involving Philemon, Onesimus, And Paul. However, Its Deeper Purpose Reveals Profound Principles About Forgiveness, Reconciliation, And The Nature Of Christian Relationships. Let Us Explore These Purposes In Detail.

## 1. To Reconcile Philemon And Onesimus

The Immediate Purpose Of The Letter Is To Bring About Reconciliation Between Philemon And Onesimus, A Runaway Slave Who Has Now Become A Fellow Believer In Christ. Paul Writes To Philemon Not Merely To Encourage Forgiveness But To Urge Him To Restore And Transform His Relationship With Onesimus.

Paul's Appeal Is Grounded In The Teachings Of Jesus, Particularly The Importance Of Forgiveness (Matthew 6:14-15). In Philemon 1:16-17, Paul Asks Philemon To Welcome Onesimus "No Longer As A Slave, But Better Than A Slave, As A Dear Brother." This Reflects The Christian Principle That In Christ, Relationships Are Renewed And Transcended By The Unity Of The Faith.

**Connecting Verses:**

- 2 Corinthians 5:18-19: Paul Explains That God Reconciled Us To Himself Through Christ And Entrusted Believers With The Ministry Of Reconciliation, A Theme That Underpins His Letter To Philemon.
- Colossians 3:13: This Verse Exhorts Christians To Forgive As The Lord Forgave Them, Providing The Moral Foundation For Philemon's Forgiveness Of Onesimus.
- Matthew 18:21-22: Jesus Teaches That Forgiveness Should Be Limitless, Illustrating The Depth Of Grace Expected In Christian Relationships.

Reconciliation Is Not Merely The Resolution Of A Dispute But A Demonstration Of The Transformative Power Of The Gospel. By Urging Philemon To Forgive And Welcome Onesimus As A Brother, Paul Models The Redemptive Work Of Christ.

## 2. To Illustrate The Transformative Power Of The Gospel

A Central Purpose Of The Letter Is To Highlight The Gospel's Power To Transform Individuals And Relationships. Onesimus, Whose Name Means "Useful," Is Described By Paul As Having Become Truly Useful Through His Faith In Christ (Philemon 1:10-11). This Transformation Is A Testament To The Renewing Work Of The Holy Spirit.

Paul's Letter Also Demonstrates How The Gospel Redefines Societal Norms. In The Roman World, Slaves Were Considered Property, Yet Paul Urges Philemon To Treat Onesimus As A Beloved Brother. This Reflects The Radical Equality And Unity Of Believers In Christ, As Expressed In Galatians 3:28.

**Connecting Verses:**

- 2 Corinthians 5:17: "If Anyone Is In Christ, The New Creation Has Come: The Old Has Gone, The New Is Here!" This Verse Encapsulates The Transformation Seen In Onesimus.
- Romans 12:2: Believers Are Called To Be Transformed By The Renewing Of Their Minds, A Principle Evident In The Changed Relationship Between Philemon And Onesimus.
- Ephesians 2:14-16: Christ's Work On The Cross Breaks Down Barriers And Creates Unity, Mirroring The Reconciliation Paul Envisions Between Philemon And Onesimus.

The Letter Serves As A Living Example Of How Faith In Christ Transforms Every Aspect Of Life, Including Deeply Entrenched Social Structures.

## *3. To Model Christian Leadership And Mediation*

Another Purpose Of The Letter Is To Provide An Example Of Christian Leadership. Paul Does Not Command Philemon To Forgive Onesimus But Appeals To Him "Based On Love" (Philemon 1:9). This Approach Reflects Humility And Respect, Qualities That Are Essential In Christian Leadership.

Paul's Role As A Mediator Mirrors The Intercessory Work Of Christ, Who Reconciles Humanity To God (1 Timothy 2:5). By Offering To Take On Any Debts Onesimus Owes (Philemon 1:18-19), Paul Demonstrates Selflessness And Grace, Setting An Example For Believers To Follow.

**Connecting Verses:**

- John 15:13: "Greater Love Has No One Than This: To Lay Down One's Life For One's Friends." Paul's Willingness To Bear Onesimus' Burden Reflects This Sacrificial Love.
- Isaiah 53:4-6: This Prophetic Passage Describes Christ's Role As A Mediator Who Bears The Sins Of Others, A Role Paul Emulates In This Letter.
- Galatians 6:2: "Carry Each Other's Burdens, And In This Way, You Will Fulfill The Law Of Christ." Paul's Actions Embody This Principle.

Through His Example, Paul Teaches That Leadership Is Rooted In Love, Humility, And A Willingness To Serve Others.

## *4. To Model Christ-Like Mediation And Intercession*

Paul's Role As A Mediator Between Philemon And Onesimus Reflects The Work Of Christ As A Mediator For Humanity. By Offering To Repay Any Debt Owed By Onesimus (Philemon 1:18-19), Paul Embodies The Sacrificial Love Of Jesus, Who Took Upon Himself The Sins Of The World (Isaiah 53:4-6; 1 Peter 2:24).

This Act Of Mediation Not Only Resolves The Immediate Conflict But Also Points To The Greater Reconciliation Accomplished Through Christ. Paul's Willingness To Bear Onesimus' Burden Mirrors The Selfless Love Described In John 15:13: "Greater Love Has No One Than This: To Lay Down One's Life For One's Friends."

**Connecting Verses:**

- 1 Timothy 2:5: "For There Is One God And One Mediator Between God And Mankind, The Man Christ Jesus."
- Galatians 6:2: Paul Instructs Believers To "Carry Each Other's Burdens," Exemplifying This Principle In His Advocacy For Onesimus.

By Acting As A Mediator, Paul Teaches A Practical Lesson In Peacemaking And Christ-like love, Encouraging Believers To Seek Reconciliation And Unity In Their Relationships.

## 5. *To Strengthen The Early Christian Community*

Finally, The Letter To Philemon Serves To Strengthen The Bonds Of The Early Christian Community By Exemplifying The Practical Application Of Gospel Principles. Paul Addresses Not Only Philemon But Also Apphia, Archippus, And The Church That Meets In Their Home (Philemon 1:2). This Communal Aspect Underscores The Importance Of Accountability And Mutual Support Within The Body Of Christ.

The Reconciliation Between Philemon And Onesimus Would Have Served As A Powerful Witness To The Transformative Power Of The Gospel Within The Christian Community. By Extending Grace And Forgiveness, Philemon Would Have Demonstrated The Love Of Christ To Those Around Him, Encouraging Others To Do The Same.

**Connecting Verses:**

- Hebrews 10:24-25: Believers Are Encouraged To Spur One Another On Toward Love And Good Deeds, Reflecting The Communal Aspect Of Faith Seen In Philemon.
- Ephesians 4:1-3: Paul's Call To Unity, Humility, And Love Within The Body Of Christ Resonates With The Message Of This Letter.

The Letter's Emphasis On Community And Mutual Accountability Remains A Vital Lesson For Modern Believers, Reminding Us Of The Importance Of Living Out Our Faith In Fellowship With Others.

# CHAPTER TWO

# CHAPTER-BY-CHAPTER EXPLANATION

## A. PHILEMON 1:1-3 - PAUL'S GREETING

*Verse 1:*

**"Paul, A Prisoner Of Christ Jesus, And Timothy Our Brother, To Philemon Our Dear Friend And Fellow Worker..."**

Paul Begins His Letter By Introducing Himself Not As An Apostle, Which He Often Does In His Other Epistles, But As A "Prisoner Of Christ Jesus." This Deliberate Choice Of Words Sets A Humble Tone, Emphasizing His Physical Imprisonment For The Sake Of The Gospel And His Spiritual Submission To Christ.

Paul Includes Timothy In The Greeting, Who Is Not Co-Authoring But Is A Fellow Worker And Trusted Companion In Ministry. This Reflects The Communal Nature Of The Early Church And The Shared Responsibility Of Spreading The Gospel.

Philemon Is Addressed As A "Dear Friend And Fellow Worker." This Highlights The Personal Nature Of The Letter And Paul's

Respect For Philemon's Faith And Contributions To The Christian Community. The Description "Fellow Worker" Indicates That Philemon Was Actively Involved In Ministry, Possibly Hosting A Church In His Home (As Seen Later In Verse 2).

**Connecting Verses:**

- Ephesians 3:1: Paul Similarly Refers To Himself As A Prisoner Of Christ, Highlighting His Willingness To Suffer For The Sake Of The Gospel.
- 2 Timothy 2:3: Paul Exhorts Timothy To Join Him In Suffering For Christ, Reflecting The Shared Commitment Of Early Christian Leaders.
- Romans 16:3: Paul Uses Similar Language To Describe Priscilla And Aquila As "Fellow Workers," Underscoring The Value Of Partnership In Ministry.

Paul's Greeting Here Also Sets The Tone For The Entire Letter, Emphasizing Humility, Love, And Mutual Respect—Qualities That Will Underpin His Later Appeal To Philemon On Behalf Of Onesimus.

## *Verse 2:*

### *"Also, To Apphia Our Sister And Archippus Our Fellow Soldier—And To The Church That Meets In Your Home..."*

Paul Expands His Address To Include Apphia, Likely Philemon's Wife, And Archippus, Possibly Philemon's Son Or A Leader In The Church. By Mentioning Them, Paul Acknowledges The Household Dynamic And The Interconnectedness Of Their Roles Within The Christian Community.

The Mention Of "The Church That Meets In Your Home" Highlights The Early Christian Practice Of House Churches. This

Setting Reflects The Simplicity And Intimacy Of Worship In The First-Century Church, Where Believers Gathered In Private Homes To Share Fellowship, Study Scripture, And Worship Together (Acts 2:46).

The Phrase "Fellow Soldier" Used For Archippus Suggests A Sense Of Spiritual Warfare And Steadfastness In The Faith. This Metaphor Is Often Used By Paul To Describe The Dedication And Perseverance Required In Ministry.

**Connecting Verses:**

- Colossians 4:17: Paul Specifically Addresses Archippus, Urging Him To Fulfill The Ministry He Received In The Lord, Which Reinforces His Role As A Committed Leader.
- 1 Corinthians 16:19: Priscilla And Aquila Are Similarly Described As Hosting A Church In Their Home, Reflecting The Importance Of Household-Centered Ministry In The Early Church.
- 2 Timothy 2:3-4: Paul Calls Timothy To Endure Hardship Like A Good Soldier Of Christ, Aligning With The Image Of Archippus As A "Fellow Soldier."

This Verse Underscores The Communal And Familial Nature Of The Early Church, Where Entire Households Were Involved In The Work Of The Gospel. It Also Highlights The Need For Cooperation And Shared Responsibility In Building The Christian Community.

## *Verse 3:*

### *"Grace To You And Peace From God Our Father And The Lord Jesus Christ."*

As Is Customary In Paul's Letters, He Begins With A Blessing Of Grace And Peace. These Two Terms Encapsulate The Essence Of The Gospel Message: Grace Represents God's Unmerited Favor,

While Peace Signifies The Reconciliation And Harmony Brought About Through Christ.

The Dual Source Of This Blessing—"God Our Father And The Lord Jesus Christ"—Affirms The Divine Nature Of Christ And The Unity Of The Father And Son. Paul's Greeting Serves As A Reminder Of The Spiritual Blessings Available To Believers Through Their Relationship With God.

**Connecting Verses:**

- Romans 1:7: Paul Uses A Similar Greeting, Emphasizing The Universality Of Grace And Peace As Gifts From God To All Believers.
- Ephesians 2:8: The Concept Of Grace As A Gift From God Is Central To Paul's Theology, Underscoring Salvation As A Result Of God's Favor, Not Human Effort.
- John 14:27: Jesus Promises His Peace To His Disciples, A Peace That Is Not Of The World But Rooted In Him.

This Verse Encapsulates The Heart Of Paul's Message: The Transformative Power Of God's Grace And The Resulting Peace That Characterizes The Christian Life. It Serves As A Foundation For The Themes Of Forgiveness And Reconciliation That Will Unfold In The Letter.

## *Summary Of Verses 1-3*

The Opening Verses Of Philemon Establish The Tone And Context Of The Letter. They Reflect Paul's Humility, Emphasize The Communal Nature Of The Early Church, And Affirm The Centrality Of Grace And Peace In The Christian Faith. These Verses Are Not Merely Formalities; They Are Rich With Theological Significance And Lay The Groundwork For Paul's Later Appeal To Philemon On Behalf Of Onesimus.

# B. PHILEMON 1:4 -7 PAUL'S THANKSGIVING AND AFFIRMATION

*Verse 4:*

### *"I Always Thank My God As I Remember You In My Prayers..."*

Paul Begins This Section With A Heartfelt Expression Of Gratitude For Philemon. This Thanksgiving Highlights The Apostle's Prayerful Relationship With Those In The Christian Community. Paul's Consistent Prayers For Philemon Reveal His Deep Love And Care For Him As A Friend, Brother, And Fellow Worker In Christ.

Paul Often Begins His Letters With A Similar Tone Of Thanksgiving, Showing His Appreciation For The Work Of God In The Lives Of Others. This Practice Underscores The Importance Of Gratitude And Intercession In Christian Relationships.

**Connecting Verses:**

- Philippians 1:3-4: Paul Similarly Expresses His Gratitude And Constant Prayers For The Believers In Philippi, Reflecting His Consistent Practice Of Prayerful Thanksgiving.
- 1 Thessalonians 5:16-18: Paul Encourages Believers To "Pray Continually" And "Give Thanks In All Circumstances," Modeling This In His Letter To Philemon.
- Ephesians 1:15-16: Paul's Prayers Of Thanksgiving For The Ephesian Church Parallel His Prayers For Philemon, Emphasizing The Communal Nature Of Faith.

Paul's Example Challenges Believers To Cultivate A Heart Of Gratitude And To Regularly Lift Others In Prayer, Recognizing God's Work In Their Lives.

## *Verse 5:*

### *"Because I Hear About Your Love For All His Holy People And Your Faith In The Lord Jesus."*

Paul Commends Philemon For His Faith In Jesus And His Love For Fellow Believers. This Verse Ties Together Two Central Aspects Of The Christian Life: Love And Faith. Paul Acknowledges Philemon's Reputation For Embodying These Virtues, Which Serves As A Foundation For His Later Appeal On Behalf Of Onesimus.

The Phrase "Love For All His Holy People" (Or "Love For The Saints") Reflects Philemon's Active Involvement In The Christian Community. His Faith Is Not Merely Personal But Lived Out In Tangible Acts Of Love And Service To Others.

**Connecting Verses:**

- Galatians 5:6: Paul Emphasizes That Faith Is Expressed Through Love, Showing The Inseparable Connection Between The Two.
- 1 John 3:18: John Urges Believers To Love Not With Words Or Speech But With Actions And In Truth, Aligning With The Love Philemon Demonstrates.
- James 2:17: James Teaches That Faith Without Works Is Dead, Reinforcing The Active Nature Of Philemon's Faith As Described By Paul.

This Verse Highlights The Importance Of A Faith That Manifests In Love, Encouraging Believers To Reflect On How Their Faith Impacts Their Relationships And Actions.

## *Verse 6:*

### *"I Pray That Your Partnership With Us In The Faith May Be Effective In Deepening Your Understanding Of Every Good Thing We Share For The Sake Of Christ."*

Paul Prays That Philemon's Partnership (Or "Fellowship") In The Faith Would Lead To A Deeper Understanding Of The Blessings Believers Share In Christ. The Word "Partnership" (Greek: Koinonia) Conveys A Sense Of Mutual Sharing And Active Participation In The Christian Community.

Paul's Prayer Emphasizes The Interconnectedness Of Faith And Knowledge, Suggesting That Spiritual Growth Occurs Through Active Engagement With Others. This Verse Also Hints At The Transformative Power Of The Gospel, Which Unites Believers And Equips Them To Live Out Their Faith In Tangible Ways.

**Connecting Verses:**

- Acts 2:42: The Early Believers Devoted Themselves To Fellowship (Koinonia), Highlighting The Communal Nature Of Faith.
- 2 Peter 1:3-4: Peter Speaks Of The "Great And Precious Promises" Believers Share In Christ, Echoing Paul's Prayer For Philemon To Grasp These Blessings.
- Ephesians 3:16-19: Paul Prays For The Ephesian Believers To Grow In Their Understanding Of Christ's Love, Similar To His Prayer For Philemon.

This Verse Calls Believers To Embrace The Communal Aspect Of Faith, Recognizing That Spiritual Growth And Understanding Are Cultivated In Partnership With Others.

*Verse 7:*

**"Your Love Has Given Me Great Joy And Encouragement, Because You, Brother, Have Refreshed The Hearts Of The Lord's People."**

Paul Concludes This Section By Affirming The Impact Of Philemon's Love On The Christian Community. His Acts Of Kindness And Generosity Have Brought Joy And Encouragement To Paul And Have "Refreshed" The Hearts Of Fellow Believers. The Imagery Of Refreshment Suggests Relief, Restoration, And Renewal—Qualities That Reflect The Transformative Power Of Christian Love.

This Commendation Not Only Celebrates Philemon's Faithfulness But Also Sets The Stage For Paul's Appeal. By Highlighting Philemon's Character, Paul Subtly Encourages Him To Extend The Same Love And Generosity To Onesimus.

**Connecting Verses:**

- Proverbs 11:25: "A Generous Person Will Prosper; Whoever Refreshes Others Will Be Refreshed." This Proverb Aligns With The Joy And Encouragement Philemon Brings To Others.
- Hebrews 10:24: Believers Are Called To Spur One Another On Toward Love And Good Deeds, A Principle Exemplified By Philemon's Actions.
- Matthew 25:40: Jesus Teaches That Acts Of Love And Kindness Toward Others Are Ultimately Acts Done Unto Him, Reinforcing The Spiritual Significance Of Philemon's Generosity.

This Verse Serves As A Reminder Of The Profound Impact That Love And Kindness Can Have Within The Christian Community, Inspiring Believers To Be A Source Of Encouragement And Refreshment To Others.

## *Summary Of Philemon 1:4-7*

In These Verses, Paul Expresses Gratitude For Philemon's Faith And Love, Prays For His Spiritual Growth, And Affirms His Impact On The Christian Community. This Section Highlights The Importance Of Living Out Faith Through Love, The Communal Nature Of Christian Fellowship, And The Joy That Comes From Serving Others. Paul's Thanksgiving And Affirmation Lay A Strong Foundation For His Forthcoming Appeal, Demonstrating The Relational And Transformative Power Of The Gospel.

# C. PHILEMON 1:8-20 – PAUL'S APPEAL FOR ONESIMUS

***Verses 8-9:***

***"Therefore, Although In Christ I Could Be Bold And Order You To Do What You Ought To Do, Yet I Prefer To Appeal To You On The Basis Of Love."***

Paul Opens His Appeal By Acknowledging The Authority He Possesses As An Apostle. He Could Command Philemon To Act By Christian Principles, But Instead, He Chooses To Appeal Out Of Love. This Choice Reflects Paul's Humility And Respect For Philemon, As Well As The Relational Nature Of His Request.

The Emphasis On Love Rather Than Authority Highlights The Transformative Power Of The Gospel, Which Calls Believers To Act Not Out Of Obligation But Out Of A Genuine Desire To Reflect Christ's Love.

**Connecting Verses:**

- Matthew 22:37-39: Jesus Teaches That Love Is The Greatest Commandment, Which Forms The Foundation Of Paul's Appeal.
- 1 Corinthians 13:1-3: Paul Emphasizes That Actions Without Love Are Meaningless, Underscoring The Importance Of Love In Christian Relationships.
- Galatians 5:13: Paul Encourages Believers To Serve One Another Humbly In Love, A Principle He Models In His Approach To Philemon.

Paul's Appeal Challenges Believers To Reflect On Their Own Motivations, Urging Them To Act Out Of Love Rather Than Obligation.

## *Verses 10-11:*

***"I Appeal To You For My Son Onesimus, Who Became My Son While I Was In Chains. Formerly He Was Useless To You, But Now He Has Become Useful Both To You And To Me."***

Paul Refers To Onesimus As His "Son," Indicating The Deep Spiritual Bond They Share Through Onesimus' Conversion To Christianity. This Transformation Is The Crux Of Paul's Appeal—Onesimus, Once A Runaway And Potentially "Useless" Servant, Has Now Become A Valuable Member Of The Christian Community.

The Play On The Name Onesimus, Which Means "Useful," Highlights The Redemptive Power Of The Gospel To Restore Identity And Purpose. By Pointing Out Onesimus' Newfound Usefulness, Paul Emphasizes The Impact Of Faith On An Individual's Life And Relationships.

**Connecting Verses:**

- 2 Corinthians 5:17: "If Anyone Is In Christ, The New Creation Has Come: The Old Has Gone, The New Is Here!" This Reflects Onesimus' Transformation Through His Faith.
- Ephesians 2:10: Believers Are Created In Christ For Good Works, Which Aligns With Onesimus' New Role As A Fellow Worker In The Gospel.
- Luke 15:24: The Parable Of The Prodigal Son Mirrors Onesimus' Story, As He Was "Lost" But Is Now "Found" And Restored To The Community.

This Verse Invites Readers To Consider How The Gospel Transforms Relationships And Gives New Purpose To Individuals Who Were Once Marginalized Or Estranged.

### Verses 12-14:

*I Am Sending Him—Who Is My Very Heart—Back To You. I Would Have Liked To Keep Him With Me So That He Could Take Your Place In Helping Me While I Am In Chains For The Gospel. But I Did Not Want To Do Anything Without Your Consent..."*

Paul's Deep Affection For Onesimus Is Evident As He Describes Him As "My Very Heart." This Language Underscores The Close Bond They Share And The Emotional Weight Of Paul's Decision To Send Onesimus Back To Philemon.

By Returning Onesimus, Paul Demonstrates Respect For Philemon's Rights While Also Emphasizing The Importance Of Voluntary Reconciliation. He Wants Philemon's Response To Be Genuine And Not Coerced, Reflecting The Principle Of Free Will In Christian Relationships.

**Connecting Verses:**

- Matthew 5:23-24: Jesus Teaches The Importance Of Reconciliation Before Offering Gifts At The Altar, Echoing Paul's Emphasis On Restoring Relationships.
- Romans 14:19: Paul Encourages Believers To Pursue Peace And Mutual Edification, Which Aligns With His Goal For Philemon And Onesimus.
- Proverbs 21:1: This Verse Highlights How God Directs Hearts, Reminding Readers That Genuine Acts Of Love And Reconciliation Are Inspired By Him.

Paul's Approach Models How Believers Can Navigate Sensitive Situations With Love, Humility, And Respect For Others.

## *Verses 15-16:*

*"Perhaps The Reason He Was Separated From You For A Little While Was That You Might Have Him Back Forever—No Longer As A Slave, But Better Than A Slave, As A Dear Brother."*

Here, Paul Frames Onesimus' Departure And Return Within The Providence Of God. He Suggests That Onesimus' Temporary Separation From Philemon Served A Greater Purpose: To Reunite Them As Brothers In Christ. This Perspective Reflects The Overarching Theme Of God's Sovereignty In Orchestrating Events For His Glory And The Good Of His People (Romans 8:28).

Paul's Statement Challenges The Societal Norms Of His Time By Elevating Onesimus' Status From A Slave To A Beloved Brother. This Redefinition Of Their Relationship Underscores The Equality And Unity That The Gospel Brings To All Believers.

**Connecting Verses:**

- Genesis 50:20: Joseph Acknowledges God's Sovereignty In Turning Evil Intentions Into Good, Paralleling Paul's Perspective On Onesimus' Journey.
- Galatians 3:28: In Christ, All Distinctions Are Dissolved, Reinforcing Paul's Appeal For Onesimus To Be Treated As An Equal.
- 1 Peter 2:16: Believers Are Called To Live As Free People, Serving God And Reflecting His Values In Their Relationships.

This Verse Calls Readers To View Their Relationships Through The Lens Of The Gospel, Recognizing The Spiritual Bond That Unites All Believers.

## *Verses 17-18:*

### *"So, If You Consider Me A Partner, Welcome Him As You Would Welcome Me. If He Has Done You Any Wrong Or Owes You Anything, Charge It To Me."*

Paul Makes A Bold Request For Philemon To Receive Onesimus With The Same Warmth And Respect He Would Extend To Paul Himself. This Appeal Reflects The Profound Unity And Love That Should Characterize Christian Relationships.

Paul's Willingness To Take On Onesimus' Debts Mirrors Christ's Sacrificial Act On The Cross, Where He Bore The Sins Of Humanity To Reconcile Us To God (2 Corinthians 5:21). This Act Of Mediation Exemplifies The Selflessness And Grace That Believers Are Called To Embody.

**Connecting Verses:**

- Matthew 25:40: Jesus Teaches That Acts Of Kindness Toward Others Are Ultimately Acts Done Unto Him, Echoing Paul's Request To Welcome Onesimus As He Would Welcome Paul.
- Isaiah 53:4-6: The Prophetic Description Of Christ Bearing The Burden Of Humanity's Sins Parallels Paul's Willingness To Assume Onesimus' Debts.
- Galatians 6:2: Believers Are Called To Carry One Another's Burdens; A Principal Paul Demonstrates In His Advocacy For Onesimus.

This Verse Challenges Readers To Consider How They Can Extend Grace And Forgiveness To Others, Reflecting Christ's Love In Their Relationships.

## *Verses 19-20:*

*I, Paul, Am Writing This With My Own Hand. I Will Pay It Back—Not To Mention That You Owe Me Your Very Self. I Do Wish, Brother, That I May Have Some Benefit From You In The Lord; Refresh My Heart In Christ."*

Paul Concludes His Appeal With A Personal Touch, Emphasizing His Sincerity And Commitment By Writing In His Hand. His Statement About Philemon Owing Him His "Very Self" Likely Refers To Paul's Role In Philemon's Spiritual Journey, Highlighting The Debt Of Gratitude Philemon Owes.

The Phrase "Refresh My Heart In Christ" Echoes Paul's Earlier Commendation Of Philemon (Verse 7). By Granting Paul's Request, Philemon Would Not Only Demonstrate His Love And Faith But Also Bring Joy And Encouragement To Paul.

**Connecting Verses:**

- 1 Corinthians 9:11: Paul Reminds The Corinthians Of The Spiritual Benefits They Have Received Through His Ministry, Similar To His Reminder To Philemon.
- Matthew 18:27-33: The Parable Of The Unforgiving Servant Underscores The Importance Of Extending The Same Grace We Have Received From God To Others.
- Philippians 2:1-2: Paul Encourages Believers To Bring Him Joy By Being United In Love And Purpose, Aligning With His Request To Philemon.

This Verse Serves As A Powerful Reminder Of The Interconnectedness Of Faith, Love, And Gratitude In The Christian Life.

## *Summary Of Philemon 1:8-20*

In This Section, Paul Makes A Heartfelt Appeal For Onesimus, Highlighting Themes Of Reconciliation, Forgiveness, And The Transformative Power Of The Gospel. His Christ-Like Mediation, Grounded In Love And Humility, Serves As A Model For Believers To Follow In Their Own Relationships. Paul's Words Challenge Readers To Embrace The Radical Equality And Unity That The Gospel Brings, Extending Grace And Love To All.

# D. PHILEMON 1:21-25 –

# FINAL ENCOURAGEMENT, GREETINGS, AND BLESSING

*Verse 21:*

*"Confident Of Your Obedience, I Write To You, Knowing That You Will Do Even More Than I Ask."*

Paul Expresses Confidence In Philemon's Willingness To Act According To His Request, Not Just Fulfilling The Minimum Expectations But Going Beyond Them. This Statement Reflects Paul's Trust In Philemon's Faith, Love, And Character As A Mature Believer.

By Framing His Request In This Way, Paul Not Only Encourages Philemon But Also Sets A High Standard For Him To Live Up To. This Verse Also Hints At The Transformative Nature Of The Gospel, Which Calls Believers To Act With Generosity, Grace, And Love.

**Connecting Verses:**

- Matthew 5:41: Jesus Teaches His Disciples To Go The Extra Mile, Embodying The Principle Of Doing More Than What Is Required.
- 2 Corinthians 9:7: Paul Emphasizes Cheerful And Wholehearted Giving, Aligning With His Confidence That Philemon Will Respond With Love And Generosity.

- Ephesians 3:20: God Is Able To Do Immeasurably More Than We Ask Or Imagine, A Principle Reflected In Paul's Faith That Philemon Will Exceed Expectations.

Paul's Confidence Serves As Both An Encouragement And A Gentle Challenge For Philemon, Urging Him To Fully Embody The Gospel In His Response To Onesimus.

## Verse 22:

### "And One Thing More: Prepare A Guest Room For Me, Because I Hope To Be Restored To You In Answer To Your Prayers."

Paul's Request For A Guest Room Underscores His Personal Connection To Philemon And His Hope For Future Fellowship. It Also Reflects Paul's Trust In The Power Of Prayer, As He Mentions His Expectation Of Being Released From Imprisonment In Response To The Prayers Of Philemon And Others.

This Verse Reminds Readers Of The Importance Of Hospitality Within The Christian Community, As Well As The Role Of Prayer In Sustaining And Supporting One Another.

**Connecting Verses:**

- Hebrews 13:2: Believers Are Encouraged To Show Hospitality, Reflecting The Communal Care Emphasized By Paul's Request For Lodging.
- Colossians 4:3-4: Paul Asks The Colossians To Pray For His Release, Demonstrating His Reliance On The Prayers Of Others.
- James 5:16: The Prayer Of A Righteous Person Is Powerful And Effective, Aligning With Paul's Confidence In The Prayers Of Philemon And The Church.

Paul's Hope For Restoration Highlights The Relational Nature Of His Ministry, Emphasizing The Value Of Fellowship And Mutual Encouragement Among Believers.

## *Verses 23-24:*

### *"Epaphras, My Fellow Prisoner In Christ Jesus, Sends You Greetings. And So Do Mark, Aristarchus, Demas, And Luke, My Fellow Workers."*

Paul Includes Greetings From His Companions, Emphasizing The Interconnectedness Of The Early Christian Community. These Individuals Played Significant Roles In The Spread Of The Gospel, And Their Mention Serves To Encourage And Affirm Philemon's Involvement In The Shared Mission.

i. Epaphras: Likely A Leader In The Colossian Church (Colossians 4:12-13), Epaphras Is Described As A "Fellow Prisoner," Indicating His Dedication To The Gospel Despite Personal Cost.
ii. Mark: Also Known As John Mark, He Was A Companion Of Paul And Barnabas (Acts 12:25) And Later The Author Of The Gospel Of Mark.
iii. Aristarchus: A Faithful Companion Of Paul, Mentioned In Acts 19:29 And Acts 27:2.
iv. Demas: Initially A Co-Worker Of Paul But Later Mentioned As Having Deserted Him (2 Timothy 4:10), Highlighting The Challenges Of Ministry.
v. Luke: The Beloved Physician (Colossians 4:14) And Author Of The Gospel Of Luke And Acts, Who Accompanied Paul On Many Of His Journeys

**Connecting Verses:**

- Romans 16:3-16: Paul Often Includes Greetings In His Letters, Reflecting The Relational And Communal Nature Of Early Christianity.
- 2 Timothy 4:11: Paul Mentions Mark And Luke Again, Indicating Their Enduring Roles In His Ministry.
- 1 Corinthians 12:12-14: The Body Of Christ Is Made Up Of Many Parts, Emphasizing The Diverse Contributions Of Each Individual Within The Community.

The Inclusion Of These Names Reinforces The Idea That The Christian Life Is Not Lived In Isolation But Within A Network Of Relationships And Shared Purpose.

## *Verse 25:*

## *"The Grace Of The Lord Jesus Christ Be With Your Spirit."*

Paul Concludes His Letter With A Blessing Of Grace, A Hallmark Of His Epistolary Style. By Invoking The Grace Of The Lord Jesus Christ, Paul Points To The Foundation Of The Christian Life: God's Unmerited Favor And The Transformative Power Of Christ's Work.

This Final Blessing Serves As A Reminder Of The Spiritual Resources Available To Philemon As He Considers Paul's Request. It Also Connects The Letter's Themes Of Forgiveness, Reconciliation, And Love To The Overarching Message Of The Gospel.

**Connecting Verses:**

- Romans 16:20: Paul Concludes With A Similar Blessing Of Grace, Highlighting Its Centrality In His Letters.
- 2 Corinthians 13:14: The Grace Of Jesus Is Paired With The Love Of God And Fellowship Of The Holy Spirit, Emphasizing The Fullness Of God's Blessings.

- Ephesians 2:8-9: Grace Is Described As The Means Of Salvation, A Foundational Truth That Underpins Paul's Message To Philemon.

This Closing Verse Leaves Readers With A Sense Of Hope And Encouragement, Reminding Them Of The Sustaining Power Of God's Grace In Their Lives And Relationships.

## *Summary Of Philemon 1:21-25*

These Verses Bring Paul's Letter To A Close, Reinforcing The Themes Of Trust, Fellowship, And Grace. Paul's Confidence In Philemon, His Acknowledgment Of The Christian Community, And His Final Blessing All Point To The Transformative Power Of The Gospel. This Section Encourages Believers To Act With Faith, Love, And Generosity, Trusting In God's Grace To Guide And Empower Their Actions.

# THEOLOGICAL INSIGHTS

## A. LESSONS ON RECONCILIATION AND FORGIVENESS

### RECONCILIATION IN THE BOOK OF PHILEMON

## 1. Reconciliation Rooted In The Gospel

Reconciliation Is The Central Theme Of Philemon. Paul Appeals To Philemon To Reconcile With Onesimus, Who Was Once His Slave But Has Now Become A Fellow Believer. Paul Urges Philemon To See Onesimus Not As Property But As A "Beloved Brother" In Christ (Philemon 1:16). This Radical Redefinition Of Their Relationship Is Grounded In The Gospel, Which Reconciles All Believers To God And One Another.

- 2 Corinthians 5:18-19: "God... Reconciled Us To Himself Through Christ And Gave Us The Ministry Of Reconciliation." Paul's Appeal To Philemon Reflects This Divine Mission Of Restoring Broken Relationships.

- Colossians 1:19-20: Through Christ, God Reconciles "All Things" To Himself, Making Peace Through The Blood Of The Cross. This Broad Cosmic Reconciliation Sets The Foundation For Interpersonal Harmony Among Believers.

The Book Of Philemon Reminds Us That Reconciliation Is Not Just A Spiritual Concept But A Practical Reality That Transforms How We Relate To One Another.

## 2. God's Sovereignty In Reconciliation

Paul Frames Onesimus's Departure And Return As Part Of God's Providential Plan, Saying, "Perhaps The Reason He Was Separated From You For A Little While Was That You Might Have Him Back Forever" (Philemon 1:15). This Statement Underscores God's Sovereignty In Orchestrating Events For His Purposes.

- Genesis 50:20: Joseph's Declaration, "You Intended To Harm Me, But God Intended It For Good," Mirrors Paul's Perspective On Onesimus' Journey.
- Romans 8:28: "In All Things God Works For The Good Of Those Who Love Him," Assuring That God Is At Work Even In Difficult Circumstances.

Through Reconciliation, The Book Of Philemon Reveals How God's Sovereign Hand Brings About Restoration And Unity In Seemingly Hopeless Situations.

## 3. Reconciliation As A Witness To The Gospel

Paul's Appeal To Philemon Is More Than A Personal Request; It Is A Demonstration Of The Gospel's Transformative Power. By Reconciling With Onesimus, Philemon Would Reflect The Love, Unity, And Forgiveness Found In Christ.

- John 13:35: Jesus Says, "By This Everyone Will Know That You Are My Disciples, If You Love One Another." Reconciliation Between Philemon And Onesimus Would Serve As A Powerful Witness To The Christian Community.
- Matthew 5:23-24: Jesus Emphasizes The Importance Of Reconciliation, Teaching That Restoring Relationships Should Precede Even Acts Of Worship.

Reconciliation In The Book Of Philemon Challenges Believers To Live Out The Gospel In Their Relationships, Demonstrating Its Power To Heal And Unite.

# *FORGIVENESS IN THE BOOK OF PHILEMON*

## *1. Forgiveness As A Reflection Of God's Grace*

Paul's Letter Models Forgiveness As An Act Of Grace. By Asking Philemon To Forgive Onesimus And Welcome Him Back, Paul Underscores The Unmerited Nature Of Forgiveness, Mirroring God's Forgiveness Of Humanity.

- Colossians 3:13: "Forgive As The Lord Forgave You." This Direct Command Ties Human Forgiveness To Divine Forgiveness, Reminding Us That The Grace We Extend To Others Reflects God's Grace Toward Us.
- Ephesians 4:32: "Be Kind And Compassionate To One Another, Forgiving Each Other, Just As In Christ God Forgave You." This Verse Reinforces The Call To Forgive Others As An Act Of Love And Obedience.

Through Philemon, We See That Forgiveness Is Not Based On The Offender's Worthiness But On The Forgiver's Willingness To Extend Grace.

## *2. Forgiveness And The Breaking Of Social Barriers*

The Act Of Forgiving Onesimus And Accepting Him As A Brother Was A Radical Departure From The Cultural Norms Of The Roman Empire, Where Slavery Was Deeply Entrenched. Paul's Request Challenges Philemon To Rise Above Societal Expectations And Embody The Gospel's Vision Of Equality And Unity.

- Galatians 3:28: "There Is Neither Jew Nor Gentile, Neither Slave Nor Free... For You Are All One In Christ Jesus." Forgiveness In The Christian Context Dissolves Social And Cultural Divides,

Creating A New Community Founded On Love And Grace.
- 1 Peter 2:16: Believers Are Called To Live As Free People, Showing That True Freedom In Christ Breaks The Chains Of Hierarchy And Division.

Philemon Teaches That Forgiveness Is Personal And Socially Transformative, Breaking Down Barriers And Creating Unity In The Body Of Christ.

## 3. Forgiveness As A Path To Restoration

Paul Doesn't Merely Ask For Onesimus' Forgiveness; He Advocates For Full Restoration, Urging Philemon To Welcome Him "As You Would Welcome Me" (Philemon 1:17). This Act Of Restoration Goes Beyond Forgiveness, Seeking To Rebuild The Relationship On A New Foundation Of Equality And Love.

- Luke 15:22-24: The Parable Of The Prodigal Son Illustrates The Joy Of Restoration, As The Father Not Only Forgives The Son But Also Restores Him To His Position In The Family.
- Isaiah 61:7: The Promise Of Restoration—"Instead Of Your Shame You Will Receive A Double Portion"—Reflects God's Desire To Restore What Was Broken Or Lost.

Philemon Challenges Believers To Go Beyond Forgiveness, Seeking To Fully Restore Relationships And Reflect The Reconciliation Made Possible Through Christ.

## *Intertwined Themes: The Relationship Between Reconciliation And Forgiveness*

Reconciliation And Forgiveness Are Inseparable, Each Dependent On The Other. Forgiveness Removes The Barriers Of Resentment And Bitterness, Paving The Way For Reconciliation. Reconciliation, In Turn, Brings Relationships To A Place Of Restored Unity And Peace.

Paul's Role As A Mediator Between Philemon And Onesimus Mirrors Christ's Work As The Mediator Between God And Humanity. Paul's Willingness To Take On Onesimus' Debt (Philemon 1:18-19) Reflects Christ's Sacrificial Love, Pointing To The Theological Foundation Of Forgiveness And Reconciliation.

- 1 Timothy 2:5: "For There Is One God And One Mediator Between God And Mankind, The Man Christ Jesus." Paul's Intercession Reflects This Mediating Role.
- 2 Corinthians 5:21: "God Made Him Who Had No Sin To Be Sin For Us, So That In Him We Might Become The Righteousness Of God." Paul's Willingness To Bear Onesimus' Burden Parallels Christ's Substitutionary Atonement.

Through These Intertwined Themes, The Book Of Philemon Calls Believers To Model Christ-Like Love, Extending Forgiveness And Pursuing Reconciliation In All Relationships.

## *Conclusion*

The Book Of Philemon Offers Profound Theological Lessons On Reconciliation And Forgiveness. It Teaches That Reconciliation Is Grounded In The Gospel, Forgiveness Reflects God's Grace, And Both Are Essential To Building A Christ-centred community. Paul's Letter Serves As A Timeless Reminder Of The Gospel's Transformative Power To Heal Relationships, Break Down Social

Barriers, And Unite Believers As One Family In Christ.

# B. HOW CHRISTIAN VALUES CHALLENGE SOCIETAL NORMS LIKE SLAVERY.

## *THE GOSPEL'S TRANSFORMATIVE POWER ON SOCIETAL NORMS*

### *1. The Gospel Challenges The Institution Of Slavery*

In The Roman World, Slavery Was An Accepted And Entrenched Institution. Slaves Were Considered Property, With No Rights Or Autonomy. In The Book Of Philemon, However, Paul Challenges These Norms By Reframing Onesimus' Identity. Paul Describes Onesimus Not As A Mere Slave But As A "Beloved Brother" In Christ (Philemon 1:16). This Statement Undermines The Dehumanizing Perspective Of Slavery, Emphasizing The Equality Of All Believers.

- Galatians 3:28: "There Is Neither Jew Nor Gentile, Neither Slave Nor Free... For You Are All One In Christ Jesus." This Verse Encapsulates The Radical Equality That The Gospel Brings, Erasing The Societal Distinctions Of Status And Class.
- Ephesians 6:9: Paul Addresses Masters, Urging Them To Treat Their Slaves With Fairness And Without Threats, Recognizing That Both Master And Slave Have The Same Master In Heaven.

While Paul Does Not Explicitly Call For The Abolition Of Slavery In This Letter, His Appeal For Onesimus' Acceptance As A Brother Challenges The Very Foundation Of Slavery, Laying The Groundwork For Its Eventual Rejection Within Christian Ethics.

## 2. A New Identity In Christ

The Gospel Redefines Identity, Emphasizing That All Believers Are Equal And United In Christ. Paul's Appeal To Philemon Is Rooted In This New Identity, Urging Him To See Onesimus Not Through The Lens Of Societal Norms But As A Fellow Member Of God's Family.

- 2 Corinthians 5:17: "If Anyone Is In Christ, The New Creation Has Come: The Old Has Gone, The New Is Here!" Onesimus' Transformation From A Runaway Slave To A "Useful" Brother In Christ Reflects This New Creation.
- Colossians 3:11: "Here There Is No Gentile Or Jew, Circumcised Or Uncircumcised, Barbarian, Scythian, Slave Or Free, But Christ Is All, And Is In All." This Verse Reinforces The Idea That In Christ, Social Distinctions Are Rendered Meaningless.

Paul's Letter Subtly But Powerfully Challenges The Societal Norms Of Slavery By Emphasizing That Onesimus' Worth And Identity Are No Longer Tied To His Social Status But To His Standing As A Redeemed Believer.

## 3. The Radical Love Of The Christian Community

The Christian Community, United By The Love Of Christ, Is Called To Embody Values That Often Stand In Stark Contrast To Societal Norms. Paul's Request For Philemon To Welcome Onesimus As He Would Welcome Paul Himself (Philemon 1:17) Exemplifies This Radical Love And Equality.

- John 13:34-35: Jesus Commands His Disciples To Love One Another As He Has Loved Them, Stating That This Love Will Identify Them As His Followers. Paul's Appeal To Philemon To Act Out Of Love Reflects This Command.

- 1 John 4:20-21: "Whoever Claims To Love God Yet Hates A Brother Or Sister Is A Liar... Whoever Loves God Must Also Love Their Brother And Sister." The Inclusion Of Onesimus Into The Christian Community As A Brother Demonstrates The Practical Application Of This Principle.

This Radical Love Not Only Transforms Individual Relationships But Also Serves As A Powerful Witness Against Societal Systems That Dehumanize And Oppress.

## *THEOLOGICAL THEMES IN ACTION*

### *1. Brotherhood In Christ Transcends Societal Roles*

Paul's Language In Philemon Reflects The Revolutionary Idea That Spiritual Brotherhood In Christ Supersedes Societal Roles. Onesimus, Once Considered Property, Is Now A "Beloved Brother" (Philemon 1:16). This Redefinition Of Relationships Directly Challenges The Social Hierarchies Of The Roman Empire.

- Matthew 23:8: Jesus Says, "You Are All Brothers," Emphasizing The Equal Standing Of All Believers Before God.
- Romans 12:5: "So In Christ We, Though Many, Form One Body, And Each Member Belongs To All The Others." This Verse Reinforces The Unity And Interconnectedness Of Believers, Regardless Of Social Status.

By Framing Onesimus As A Brother, Paul Calls Philemon—And The Wider Christian Community—To See Relationships Through The Lens Of The Gospel Rather Than Societal Norms.

### *2. The Gospel Undermines Oppression Without Open Rebellion*

Rather Than Directly Calling For The Abolition Of Slavery, Paul's Approach In Philemon Is Transformative And Subtle. By Appealing To Philemon's Faith And Love, Paul Encourages A Change In Perspective That Undermines The Institution Of Slavery Without Inciting Rebellion.

- Romans 12:21: "Do Not Be Overcome By Evil, But Overcome Evil With Good." Paul's Strategy Reflects This Principle, Using Love And Persuasion To Challenge Societal Norms.

- 1 Peter 2:12: Believers Are Urged To Live Such Good Lives Among The Pagans That Their Actions Lead Others To Glorify God. Paul's Appeal Models This Approach, Seeking To Transform Philemon's Actions Through The Gospel.

This Method Reflects The Power Of The Gospel To Change Hearts And Societal Structures From Within, Creating A Ripple Effect That Challenges Systems Of Oppression.

## 3. The Role Of The Christian Community In Social Transformation

The Inclusion Of Others In Paul's Letter—Apphia, Archippus, And The Church Meeting In Philemon's Home (Philemon 1:2)—Suggests That Reconciliation And The Challenge To Societal Norms Are Communal Responsibilities. The Christian Community Is Called To Support And Uphold Values That Reflect The Gospel.

- Acts 2:44-45: The Early Church Is Described As Sharing Everything In Common And Ensuring That No One Was In Need, Reflecting A Counter-Cultural Model Of Community Based On Equality And Generosity.
- Hebrews 10:24: "And Let Us Consider How We May Spur One Another On Toward Love And Good Deeds." This Verse Reinforces The Communal Aspect Of Living Out Gospel Values.

By Addressing The Entire Church, Paul Emphasizes That The Transformation Of Societal Norms Begins Within The Christian Community, Which Is Called To Model The Values Of God's Kingdom.

## Conclusion

The Book Of Philemon Demonstrates How Christian Values Challenge Societal Norms Like Slavery Through The

Transformative Power Of The Gospel. Paul's Appeal To Philemon To Treat Onesimus As A Brother, Rather Than As A Slave, Reflects The Radical Love, Equality, And Unity Found In Christ. While Paul Does Not Call For Outright Abolition, His Letter Lays The Theological Groundwork For Rejecting Systems Of Oppression And Embracing The Dignity And Worth Of Every Individual.

These Lessons From Philemon Continue To Inspire Believers To Confront Modern Forms Of Inequality And Injustice, Living Out The Gospel's Call To Reconciliation, Love, And Societal Transformation.

# C. PAUL'S ROLE AS A MEDIATOR REFLECTING CHRIST'S WORK.

## 1. Paul's Role As A Mediator

In Philemon, Paul Takes On The Role Of A Mediator Between Philemon And Onesimus. Onesimus, A Runaway Slave, Has Wronged Philemon. Paul Appeals To Philemon On Onesimus' Behalf, Asking Him To Forgive Onesimus And Receive Him As A Brother In Christ. Paul's Intercession Highlights The Transformative Power Of The Gospel To Mend Broken Relationships And Reflects Christ's Mediating Role In Reconciling Humanity To God.

- Philemon 1:10-11: Paul Refers To Onesimus As His "Son" And Describes The Transformation In Onesimus' Life: "Formerly He Was Useless To You, But Now He Has Become Useful Both To You And To Me." Paul's Plea Is Rooted In Onesimus' New Identity In Christ.
- Philemon 1:17: "So If You Consider Me A Partner, Welcome Him As You Would Welcome Me." Paul Positions Himself As A Substitute, Offering To Stand In Onesimus' Place.

Paul's Actions Reflect The Heart Of Christian Mediation: Standing In The Gap To Reconcile Estranged Parties.

## 2. Christ As The Ultimate Mediator

Paul's Mediation For Onesimus Echoes Christ's Work As The Ultimate Mediator Between God And Humanity. Just As Paul Intercedes For Onesimus, Offering To Assume Any Debts Or

Wrongs Onesimus Owes, Christ Intercedes For Sinners, Taking Upon Himself The Penalty For Sin.

- 1 Timothy 2:5: "For There Is One God And One Mediator Between God And Mankind, The Man Christ Jesus." This Verse Underscores Christ's Unique Role In Bridging The Gap Between A Holy God And Sinful Humanity.
- 2 Corinthians 5:21: "God Made Him Who Had No Sin To Be Sin For Us, So That In Him We Might Become The Righteousness Of God." Just As Paul Offers To Repay Onesimus' Debt (Philemon 1:18), Christ Bears The Debt Of Sin On Behalf Of Humanity.

Paul's Willingness To Take On Onesimus' Debts Reflects Christ's Sacrificial Love, Demonstrating How Believers Can Imitate Christ's Work In Their Relationships.

# _THEOLOGICAL LESSONS FROM PAUL'S MEDIATION_

## 1. Advocacy Based On Grace

Paul's Mediation Is Grounded In Grace, Not Obligation. He Appeals To Philemon "Based On Love" Rather Than Exercising His Apostolic Authority (Philemon 1:8-9). This Approach Reflects The Grace-Filled Nature Of Christ's Advocacy For Sinners.

- Romans 8:34: "Christ Jesus... Is Also Interceding For Us." Like Christ, Paul Does Not Demand Or Coerce But Appeals Out Of Love And Relationship.
- Ephesians 2:8-9: Salvation Is A Gift Of Grace, Not Something Earned. Paul's Approach To Philemon Mirrors The Grace That Believers Receive Through Christ.

Paul's Intercession Teaches That Mediation Should Be Rooted In Love And Grace, Reflecting The Character Of Christ.

## 2. Willingness To Bear The Cost

A Key Aspect Of Paul's Mediation Is His Willingness To Bear Onesimus' Debt. He Writes, "If He Has Done You Any Wrong Or Owes You Anything, Charge It To Me" (Philemon 1:18). This Act Of Assuming Another's Burden Mirrors Christ's Atoning Work On The Cross.

- Isaiah 53:4-6: "He Took Up Our Pain And Bore Our Suffering... The Punishment That Brought Us Peace Was On Him." Christ Bore Humanity's Burden To Bring Reconciliation With God.

- Galatians 6:2: "Carry Each Other's Burdens, And In This Way, You Will Fulfill The Law Of Christ." Paul's Actions Exemplify This Principle, Showing How Believers Can Reflect Christ's Sacrificial Love.

Paul's Willingness To Bear The Cost Of Onesimus' Wrongdoing Underscores The Depth Of Love And Commitment Required In Mediation.

## 3. Reconciliation Through Mediation

Paul's Ultimate Goal Is To Reconcile Philemon And Onesimus, Transforming Their Relationship From Master And Slave To Brothers In Christ (Philemon 1:16). This Reconciliation Is A Tangible Demonstration Of The Gospel's Power To Break Down Barriers And Create Unity.

- Colossians 1:20: Through Christ, God Reconciles "All Things" To Himself, Making Peace Through His Blood. Paul's Appeal Reflects This Ministry Of Reconciliation.
- Matthew 5:9: "Blessed Are The Peacemakers, For They Will Be Called Children Of God." Paul's Role As A Peacemaker Demonstrates The Christian Calling To Foster Reconciliation.

Paul's Intercession Reveals That Reconciliation Is Both A Spiritual And Relational Process, Rooted In The Transformative Work Of Christ.

# *PAUL'S MEDIATION AS A MODEL FOR BELIEVERS*

## *1. Imitating Christ's Intercession*

Paul's Actions In Philemon Provide A Practical Example Of How Believers Can Imitate Christ's Intercession In Their Own Lives. By Advocating For Onesimus, Paul Reflects Christ's Role As An Advocate For Humanity.

- 1 John 2:1: "If Anybody Does Sin, We Have An Advocate With The Father—Jesus Christ, The Righteous One." Just As Christ Pleads For Us, Believers Are Called To Intercede And Advocate For Others.

Paul's Willingness To Mediate Teaches Believers To Pursue Peace, Advocate For The Marginalized, And Reflect Christ's Love In Their Relationships.

## *2. Promoting Unity In The Body Of Christ*

Paul's Appeal For Reconciliation Emphasizes The Importance Of Unity Within The Christian Community. By Urging Philemon To Accept Onesimus As A Brother, Paul Demonstrates How The Gospel Transforms Relationships And Creates A New Community Founded On Love And Equality.

- Ephesians 4:3: "Make Every Effort To Keep The Unity Of The Spirit Through The Bond Of Peace." Paul's Mediation Promotes Unity And Harmony Within The Church.
- Galatians 3:28: "There Is Neither Jew Nor Gentile, Neither Slave Nor Free... For You Are All One In Christ Jesus." Paul's Appeal Challenges Societal Norms And Reflects The Gospel's Vision Of

Equality.

Through His Mediation, Paul Models How Believers Can Foster Unity And Reconciliation Within The Body Of Christ.

## *Conclusion*

Paul's Role As A Mediator In The Book Of Philemon Is A Profound Reflection Of Christ's Mediating Work. His Advocacy For Onesimus Demonstrates Grace, Sacrificial Love, And A Commitment To Reconciliation, All Of Which Echo The Gospel. Paul's Actions Challenge Believers To Imitate Christ In Their Relationships, Pursuing Peace, Unity, And Restoration. The Book Of Philemon Reminds Us That Mediation Is Not Merely A Practical Task But A Sacred Calling That Mirrors The Heart Of God's Redemptive Work Through Christ.

# PRACTICAL APPLICATIONS

## A. DRAWING PARALLELS TO MODERN RELATIONSHIPS AND CONFLICTS.

### *1. Practicing Forgiveness In Broken Relationships*

In Philemon, Paul's Appeal To Philemon To Forgive Onesimus Reflects The Necessity Of Forgiveness For Reconciliation. Today, Forgiveness Is Crucial For Resolving Conflicts In Personal, Professional, And Societal Relationships. Forgiveness Allows For Healing, Removes Bitterness, And Enables Relationships To Move Forward.

**Application:** Forgiveness In Personal Relationships

In Family Disputes Or Friendships, Hurt Feelings Or Unresolved Issues Can Strain Relationships. The Gospel-Centered Forgiveness Seen In Philemon Reminds Us That Holding Onto Grudges Harms Both Parties. Forgiveness Is An Act Of Grace That Reflects Christ's Love.

- Philemon 1:18-19: Paul Offers To Repay Any Debts Onesimus Owes, Mirroring The Sacrificial Forgiveness Believers Are Called To Extend To Others.
- Colossians 3:13: "Forgive As The Lord Forgave You." This Serves As A Reminder That Forgiveness Is Not Based On The Offender's Worthiness But Is A Response To God's Forgiveness Of Us.

**Example:**

When Dealing With Conflict In A Marriage, Extending Forgiveness Allows Couples To Build Trust And Intimacy. Choosing To Let Go Of Resentment Reflects The Grace Of God And Fosters Stronger, Healthier Relationships.

**Application:** Forgiveness In Professional Conflicts

In Workplaces, Misunderstandings, Mistakes, Or Misjudgments Often Lead To Conflicts. By Practicing Forgiveness, Employees And Employers Can Create A Culture Of Mutual Respect And Harmony.

- Ephesians 4:31-32: Paul Urges Believers To "Be Kind And Compassionate To One Another, Forgiving Each Other, Just As In Christ God Forgave You."

**Example:**

If A Colleague Fails To Complete Their Part Of A Project, Choosing To Forgive Instead Of Harboring Frustration Leads To Teamwork And A Collaborative Spirit.

## 2. The Role Of Mediation In Conflict Resolution

Paul's Role As A Mediator Between Philemon And Onesimus Is Central To The Story. He Intercedes, Advocates, And Seeks Reconciliation On Behalf Of Onesimus, Modeling How Christians Can Mediate In Conflicts.

**Application:** Becoming Peacemakers In Modern Conflicts

Mediation Plays A Vital Role In Resolving Disputes At Home, In Communities, Or Even Globally. As Seen In Philemon, Mediation Requires Humility, Empathy, And A Focus On Unity.

- Matthew 5:9: "Blessed Are The Peacemakers, For They Will Be Called Children Of God." This Verse Encourages Believers To Act As Agents Of Peace In All Areas Of Life.
- 2 Corinthians 5:18-19: Paul Highlights The "Ministry Of Reconciliation," Showing That Believers Are Called To Mend Broken Relationships.

**Example:**

In A Community Conflict Over Shared Resources, A Trusted Mediator Can Bring Both Sides Together To Find Common Ground, Emphasizing The Importance Of Unity And Collaboration.

**Application:** Mediation In Family Conflicts

Families Often Experience Disputes Over Inheritance, Caregiving Responsibilities, Or Personal Grievances. Acting As A Mediator, A Family Member Can Facilitate Reconciliation By Focusing On Shared Values And Love.

- Galatians 6:2: "Carry Each Other's Burdens, And In This Way, You Will Fulfill The Law Of Christ."

**Example:**

In A Sibling Conflict, Mediating With Understanding And Fairness Can Restore Familial Bonds And Foster Mutual Respect.

## 3. Breaking Down Social Barriers

Paul's Appeal To Philemon To Treat Onesimus As A Brother In Christ Rather Than A Slave Challenges Societal Norms. In Modern Contexts, The Principle Of Equality In Christ Can Be Applied To Combat Discrimination, Prejudice, And Systemic Inequalities.

**Application:** Promoting Equality In Social Interactions

The Gospel Calls Believers To Break Down Barriers Of Race, Class, And Gender, Viewing All People As Equal In God's Eyes. This Vision Of Unity Is Powerfully Demonstrated In Paul's Appeal In Philemon.

- Galatians 3:28: "There Is Neither Jew Nor Gentile, Neither Slave Nor Free, Nor Is There Male And Female, For You Are All One In Christ Jesus."
- James 2:1: "My Brothers And Sisters, Believers In Our Glorious Lord Jesus Christ Must Not Show Favoritism."

**Example:**
In The Workplace, Leaders Can Embrace Diversity By Ensuring That Opportunities Are Accessible To Everyone, Fostering An Inclusive Culture Where All Individuals Are Valued.

**Application:**Bridging Divisions In Communities
Social Divides, Whether Due To Cultural Differences Or Economic Disparities, Often Lead To Tensions. Drawing From Philemon, Believers Can Act As Bridges, Promoting Unity And Reconciliation.

- Ephesians 2:14-16: Christ's Work On The Cross Broke Down The Dividing Wall Of Hostility, Serving As A Model For Creating Unity In Diversity.

**Example:**
Initiating Dialogues Between Different Communities In A City Can Build Mutual Understanding And Respect, Reflecting The Inclusivity Of The Gospel.

## 4. Transforming Relationships Through The Gospel

Paul's Letter Demonstrates How The Gospel Redefines Relationships. Onesimus Moves From Being Philemon's Property To His Beloved Brother In Christ (Philemon 1:16). This Shift Has

Profound Implications For Modern Relationships, Challenging Believers To Prioritize Love And Mutual Respect.

**Application:** Restoring Relationships Through The Gospel

The Transformative Power Of The Gospel Can Heal Broken Friendships And Strained Family Dynamics. By Viewing Others Through The Lens Of Christ's Love, Believers Can Approach Relationships With Grace And Compassion.

- 2 Corinthians 5:17: "If Anyone Is In Christ, The New Creation Has Come: The Old Has Gone, The New Is Here!"
- Romans 12:10: "Be Devoted To One Another In Love. Honor One Another Above Yourselves."

**Example:**

A Friendship Damaged By Betrayal Can Be Restored When Both Individuals Embrace The Humility And Love Exemplified In Christ, Choosing To Rebuild The Bond On A Foundation Of Trust And Grace.

**Application:** Changing Leadership Approaches

In Leadership, Whether In Churches, Workplaces, Or Families, The Example Of Paul Encourages Leaders To Prioritize The Well-Being Of Others, Advocating For Fairness And Empathy.

- Matthew 20:26-28: Jesus Teaches That Leadership Is About Serving Others, Reflecting The Servant-Hearted Approach Paul Models.

**Example:**

A Manager Who Supports An Employee Facing Challenges, Rather Than Penalizing Them, Demonstrates Christ-Like Leadership.

## 5. *Living Out Forgiveness And Reconciliation In Society*

The Principles In Philemon Also Extend To Societal Issues, Such As Justice, Reconciliation, And Community Building. The Book Calls Believers To Actively Participate In Addressing Broken Systems And Relationships, Reflecting Christ's Redemptive Work.

**Application:** Advocating For Justice And Mercy

The Gospel Calls For Justice Tempered With Mercy, As Seen In Paul's Appeal For Onesimus' Reconciliation. This Balance Is Crucial In Societal Conflicts, Such As Restorative Justice Initiatives.

- Micah 6:8: "Act Justly And Love Mercy And Walk Humbly With Your God."

**Example:**

Restorative Justice Programs That Seek To Reconcile Offenders And Victims Reflect The Principles Of Forgiveness And Restoration Seen In Philemon.

**Application:** Building A Culture Of Grace

A Culture Of Grace, Where Mistakes Are Met With Understanding And Efforts Are Made To Restore Relationships, Reflects The Values In Philemon. This Approach Fosters Healthier Communities And Institutions.

- Hebrews 12:14: "Make Every Effort To Live In Peace With Everyone."

**Example:**

In Schools, Promoting Restorative Practices Over Punitive Measures Helps Build A Nurturing Environment For Students.

## *Conclusion*

The Book Of Philemon Provides Profound Lessons For Addressing Modern Relationships And Conflicts. It Challenges Believers To Practice Forgiveness, Act As Mediators, And Break Down Barriers, Reflecting The Transformative Power Of The Gospel In All Areas

Of Life. By Applying These Principles, We Can Foster Reconciliation, Unity, And Love In Our Personal Lives And Broader Communities.

# B. LIVING OUT FORGIVENESS IN OUR DAILY LIVES.

## 1. *Embracing Forgiveness As A Command, Not A Choice*

Paul's Appeal To Philemon To Forgive Onesimus Is Rooted In Christian Love And Obedience To Christ. Forgiveness Is Not Presented As Optional But As An Essential Act Of Grace Reflecting The Gospel. Similarly, In Our Daily Lives, Forgiveness Must Become A Conscious Decision Rooted In Our Faith, Even When It Is Difficult.

- Philemon 1:8-9: Paul Writes, "I Could Be Bold And Order You To Do What You Ought To Do, Yet I Prefer To Appeal To You On The Basis Of Love." Forgiveness Is Not Imposed By Obligation But Is An Outpouring Of Love And Obedience To Christ.
- Matthew 6:14-15: Jesus Teaches, "For If You Forgive Other People When They Sin Against You, Your Heavenly Father Will Also Forgive You. But If You Do Not Forgive Others Their Sins, Your Father Will Not Forgive Your Sins." This Reinforces Forgiveness As A Command Rooted In Our Relationship With God.

**Application:**
In Daily Life, Forgiving A Friend Or Family Member Who Has Wronged Us, Even If They Haven't Apologized, Reflects Obedience To Christ. Forgiveness Should Not Be Delayed Or Conditional, As It Mirrors God's Unconditional Forgiveness Of Us.

## *2. Seeing Others Through The Lens Of Grace*

Paul Challenges Philemon To View Onesimus Not As A Runaway Slave But As A "Beloved Brother" (Philemon 1:16). This Shift In Perspective Calls Us To Look Beyond Offenses And See Others As God Sees Them—Recipients Of His Grace And Forgiveness.

- Ephesians 4:32: "Be Kind And Compassionate To One Another, Forgiving Each Other, Just As In Christ God Forgave You." Forgiveness Requires Us To Treat Others With The Same Grace And Compassion That We Have Received.
- 2 Corinthians 5:17: "If Anyone Is In Christ, The New Creation Has Come: The Old Has Gone, The New Is Here!" Forgiveness Involves Recognizing The Transformative Work Of Christ In Others, Just As Paul Acknowledges Onesimus' New Identity.

### Application:
In Our Interactions, Seeing A Coworker Or Neighbor Who Has Hurt Us As Someone Loved By God Allows Us To Approach Them With Grace, Replacing Resentment With Kindness And Understanding.

## *3. Releasing The Burden Of Grudges*

Forgiveness, As Demonstrated In Philemon, Involves Letting Go Of Resentment And Bitterness. Paul Offers To Take On Onesimus' Debt, Removing Any Barrier That Might Hinder Reconciliation (Philemon 1:18). In The Same Way, We Are Called To Release The Burden Of Holding Grudges And To Choose Freedom Through Forgiveness.

- Hebrews 12:15: "See To It That No One Falls Short Of The Grace Of God And That No Bitter Root Grows Up To Cause Trouble And Defile Many." Unforgiveness Leads To Bitterness, Which Harms Relationships And Spiritual Growth.

- Romans 12:17-19: "Do Not Repay Anyone Evil For Evil... Do Not Take Revenge... For It Is Written: 'It Is Mine To Avenge; I Will Repay,' Says The Lord." Forgiveness Releases The Desire For Retaliation And Entrusts Justice To God.

**Application:**
When Dealing With A Misunderstanding In A Friendship, Letting Go Of Bitterness And Forgiving The Person Unconditionally Fosters Healing And Peace.

## 4. Actively Seeking Reconciliation

Forgiveness Is Not Merely An Internal Act But Often Involves Taking Steps Toward Reconciliation. Paul's Letter Demonstrates This Principle As He Intercedes For Onesimus And Facilitates Reconciliation With Philemon. Forgiveness Creates The Foundation For Rebuilding Trust And Restoring Broken Relationships.

- Matthew 5:23-24: Jesus Teaches, "If You Are Offering Your Gift At The Altar And There Remember That Your Brother Or Sister Has Something Against You, Leave Your Gift There... First Go And Be Reconciled To Them." Reconciliation Takes Priority Over Other Acts Of Worship.
- Romans 12:18: "If It Is Possible, As Far As It Depends On You, Live At Peace With Everyone." Forgiveness Leads To Actively Pursuing Peace.

**Application:**
After A Family Disagreement, Reaching Out To Reconcile—Even With Small Gestures Like A Message Or Phone Call—Demonstrates Humility And A Commitment To Restoring The Relationship.

## 5. *Forgiving With A Heart Of Humility*

Paul's Appeal On Behalf Of Onesimus Reflects Humility, As He Sets Aside His Own Status And Authority To Serve As A Mediator (Philemon 1:10-11). Similarly, Forgiveness Requires Humility, Recognizing Our Own Need For Grace And Extending The Same To Others.

- Philippians 2:3-4: "Do Nothing Out Of Selfish Ambition Or Vain Conceit. Rather, In Humility Value Others Above Yourselves."
- Luke 23:34: Jesus' Prayer, "Father, Forgive Them, For They Do Not Know What They Are Doing," Demonstrates Ultimate Humility In Forgiving Those Who Crucified Him.

### Application:

Choosing To Forgive A Spouse Or Partner After An Argument, Even When Feeling Justified In One's Own Position, Reflects Humility And Prioritizes The Relationship Over Being "Right."

## 6. *Modeling Forgiveness In Leadership*

Paul's Example As A Leader Shows How Forgiveness And Reconciliation Can Transform Not Just Individuals But Entire Communities. As A Spiritual Leader, Paul Encourages Philemon To Embrace Forgiveness, Setting An Example For The Church Meeting In Philemon's Home (Philemon 1:2).

- Colossians 3:14-15: Paul Teaches That Love And Peace Should Rule In The Hearts Of Believers, Uniting Them In Harmony And Forgiveness.
- 1 Corinthians 11:1: "Follow My Example, As I Follow The Example Of Christ." Leaders Are Called To Model Forgiveness, Inspiring Others To Do The Same.

### Application:

A Manager Who Forgives An Employee For Making A Costly Mistake And Works To Restore Their Confidence Creates A Culture Of Grace And Growth Within The Workplace.

## 7. *Forgiving As A Witness To Others*

Forgiveness Is Not Only An Act Of Obedience To God But Also A Testimony To His Transforming Grace. The Reconciliation Between Philemon And Onesimus, Witnessed By The Church, Serves As An Example Of Gospel-Centered Relationships.

- John 13:35: "By This Everyone Will Know That You Are My Disciples, If You Love One Another."
- Matthew 18:21-22: Jesus Teaches Peter To Forgive "Not Seven Times, But Seventy-Seven Times," Reflecting The Boundless Nature Of Christian Forgiveness.

**Application:**
Forgiving Someone Who Wronged You In A Public Setting, Such As At Work Or In A Community, Demonstrates The Power Of The Gospel And Inspires Others To Act With Grace.

## *Conclusion*

The Book Of Philemon Provides Practical And Powerful Insights Into Living Out Forgiveness In Our Daily Lives. By Following Paul's Example, Believers Are Called To Embrace Forgiveness As A Reflection Of God's Grace, Actively Pursue Reconciliation, And Foster Relationships That Mirror The Gospel. Forgiveness Not Only Transforms Individuals But Also Heals Communities, Pointing To The Redeeming Love Of Christ In Every Aspect Of Life.

# C. THE IMPORTANCE OF SEEING OTHERS THROUGH A LENS OF GRACE.

## *1. Recognizing The Transformative Power Of Grace*

Paul's Plea For Onesimus Highlights The Gospel's Ability To Transform Individuals. Onesimus, Once A Runaway Slave, Is Now Described As "Useful" (Philemon 1:11) And A "Beloved Brother" (Philemon 1:16). Viewing Others Through A Lens Of Grace Means Recognizing Their Potential For Transformation And Restoration Through Christ.

**Application:** Encouraging Second Chances

In Our Daily Lives, People Often Make Mistakes Or Fall Short Of Expectations. Viewing Them Through A Lens Of Grace Means Offering Second Chances And Believing In Their Capacity For Growth And Change.

- 2 Corinthians 5:17: "If Anyone Is In Christ, The New Creation Has Come: The Old Has Gone, The New Is Here!" This Verse Reminds Us That Faith Transforms People, Making Them New In Christ.
- Proverbs 24:16: "For Though The Righteous Fall Seven Times, They Rise Again." This Reflects The Resilience And Redemption Possible Through God's Grace.

**Example:**

In The Workplace, A Manager Who Views An Underperforming Employee With Grace Sees Beyond Their Shortcomings, Providing Guidance And Encouragement To Help Them Improve Rather Than Focusing Solely On Past Failures.

## 2. *Embracing Equality And Unity In Christ*

Paul's Declaration That Onesimus Is Now A Brother In Christ (Philemon 1:16) Breaks Down The Social Barrier Between Master And Slave. Seeing Others Through A Lens Of Grace Calls Believers To Look Beyond Societal Or Cultural Distinctions And Recognize The Intrinsic Worth Of Every Individual In Christ.

**Application:** Treating Everyone With Dignity

In Daily Interactions, We Often Encounter People From Diverse Backgrounds And Circumstances. Viewing Them Through Grace Means Treating Everyone With Respect And Dignity, Acknowledging Their Value As Image-Bearers Of God.

- Galatians 3:28: "There Is Neither Jew Nor Gentile, Neither Slave Nor Free, Nor Is There Male And Female, For You Are All One In Christ Jesus." This Verse Emphasizes The Equality Of All Believers In Christ.
- James 2:1: "Believers In Our Glorious Lord Jesus Christ Must Not Show Favoritism." This Reinforces The Call To Treat Others Impartially.

**Example:**

In A Church Setting, Creating An Environment Where People Of All Ages, Cultures, And Socioeconomic Statuses Feel Welcomed And Valued Reflects The Unity And Equality Modeled In Philemon.

## 3. *Forgiving Others Through The Lens Of Grace*

Forgiveness Is At The Heart Of Paul's Appeal To Philemon. By Asking Philemon To Forgive Onesimus And Receive Him With Love, Paul Demonstrates That Grace Enables Reconciliation And Restoration.

**Application:** Letting Go Of Grudges

In Personal Conflicts, Holding Grudges Can Create Bitterness And Division. Seeing Others Through Grace Allows Us To Forgive

Freely, Mirroring The Forgiveness We Have Received From God.

- Ephesians 4:32: "Be Kind And Compassionate To One Another, Forgiving Each Other, Just As In Christ God Forgave You." This Verse Connects Forgiveness To God's Grace.
- Matthew 6:14-15: Jesus Teaches That Forgiving Others Is Essential To Experiencing God's Forgiveness, Underscoring The Transformative Power Of Grace.

**Example:**

Forgiving A Family Member Who Has Wronged Us, Even If They Haven't Apologized, Demonstrates The Grace-Filled Forgiveness Modeled In Philemon.

## 4. Advocating For Others With Compassion

Paul's Mediation For Onesimus Reflects His Commitment To Advocating For Someone Who Could Not Defend Himself. Viewing Others Through Grace Inspires Us To Stand Up For Those Who Are Vulnerable Or Marginalized.

**Application:** Advocating For Justice

Injustice Often Arises From A Lack Of Grace-Filled Perspectives. By Seeing Others Through Christ's Lens, Believers Are Called To Advocate For Fairness And Equity.

- Micah 6:8: "Act Justly And Love Mercy And Walk Humbly With Your God." This Verse Calls For Justice Tempered With Mercy.
- Isaiah 1:17: "Learn To Do Right; Seek Justice. Defend The Oppressed."

**Example:**

Supporting A Colleague Who Is Unfairly Criticized Or Overlooked Demonstrates A Grace-Filled Approach That Seeks Justice And Compassion.

## 5. *Offering Reconciliation In Broken Relationships*

Paul Encourages Philemon To Reconcile With Onesimus, Transforming Their Relationship Into One Of Brotherhood. Living With A Lens Of Grace Means Seeking Reconciliation And Striving To Heal Broken Relationships.

**Application:** Pursuing Peace And Harmony

Grace Compels Us To Mend Strained Relationships, Even When It Requires Humility And Vulnerability. Viewing Others As Equally In Need Of God's Grace Helps Foster Peace.

- Romans 12:18: "If It Is Possible, As Far As It Depends On You, Live At Peace With Everyone." This Verse Calls For Active Efforts To Reconcile With Others.
- Matthew 5:9: "Blessed Are The Peacemakers, For They Will Be Called Children Of God." Peacemaking Reflects The Heart Of A Grace-Filled Life.

**Example:** Reaching Out To An Estranged Friend To Rebuild Trust And Communication Embodies The Gospel's Call To Reconciliation.

## 6. *Encouraging Growth And Redemption*

Paul's Letter Emphasizes Onesimus' Transformation Through Christ And His Potential To Contribute Meaningfully To The Christian Community. Seeing Others Through A Lens Of Grace Involves Encouraging Their Spiritual Growth And Supporting Their Redemption.

**Application:** Mentoring And Discipleship

In Relationships, Extending Grace Means Nurturing Others In Their Faith Journey, Offering Guidance, And Believing In Their Potential To Grow.

- Proverbs 27:17: "As Iron Sharpens Iron, So One Person Sharpens Another." Grace Inspires Mutual Growth And Edification.
- Hebrews 10:24: "Let Us Consider How We May Spur One Another On Toward Love And Good Deeds."

**Example:**

Mentoring A Young Believer Who Struggles With Their Faith, Offering Encouragement Instead Of Judgment, Fosters Their Spiritual Development.

## 7. Being Patient With Others' Flaws

Paul's Acknowledgment Of Onesimus' Previous Failings ("Formerly He Was Useless," Philemon 1:11) Is Balanced By His Recognition Of Onesimus' Transformation. A Lens Of Grace Allows Us To Be Patient With Others, Understanding That Growth Is A Process.

**Application:** Exercising Patience In Daily Interactions

Seeing Others Through Grace Means Being Patient With Their Imperfections, Trusting God's Work In Their Lives.

- Romans 15:1: "We Who Are Strong Ought To Bear With The Failings Of The Weak And Not To Please Ourselves."
- Philippians 1:6: "He Who Began A Good Work In You Will Carry It On To Completion Until The Day Of Christ Jesus."

**Example:**

When Dealing With A Coworker Who Frequently Makes Mistakes, Responding With Patience And Encouragement Rather Than Frustration Reflects Grace.

## Conclusion

The Book Of Philemon Challenges Believers To View Others Through A Lens Of Grace, Transforming How We Approach Relationships, Resolve Conflicts, And Build Community. By

Following Paul's Example And Reflecting Christ's Love, We Can See Beyond Flaws And Failures, Recognizing The Value, Potential, And Dignity Of Every Individual. This Grace-Filled Perspective Fosters Reconciliation, Unity, And A Deeper Understanding Of God's Transformative Power In Our Lives And The Lives Of Those Around Us.

# CONCLUSION

## A. SUMMARIZING THE ENDURING RELEVANCE OF PHILEMON.

### *A Model For Christian Relationships*

At Its Core, Philemon Is A Letter About Relationships Transformed By The Gospel. Paul's Appeal To Philemon To Forgive And Reconcile With Onesimus Underscores The Importance Of Viewing Others Through The Lens Of Grace And Love.

### *Relevance Today:*

### *1. Forgiveness:*

The Letter Emphasizes The Centrality Of Forgiveness In Christian Relationships. Paul's Intercession For Onesimus Reflects The Call For Believers To Reconcile With Those Who Have Wronged Them. In A World Often Marred By Grudges And Divisions, Philemon Challenges Us To Forgive Freely And Restore Broken Relationships.

- Matthew 6:14-15: Jesus Teaches That Forgiveness Is Essential For Believers To Receive God's Forgiveness.
- Ephesians 4:32: "Be Kind And Compassionate To One Another, Forgiving Each Other, Just As In Christ God Forgave You."

• 77 •

## 2. *Reconciliation:*

Philemon Highlights The Gospel's Power To Heal Relationships And Bring Unity. Paul's Role As A Mediator Calls Believers To Actively Pursue Peace And Reconciliation In Their Lives.

- 2 Corinthians 5:18-19: God Gives Believers The Ministry Of Reconciliation, Reflecting His Work In Reconciling Humanity To Himself.
- Romans 12:18: "If It Is Possible, As Far As It Depends On You, Live At Peace With Everyone."

## _A Vision Of Equality In Christ_

Philemon Redefines The Relationship Between Philemon And Onesimus, Urging Philemon To Accept Onesimus Not As A Slave But As A Brother In Christ (Philemon 1:16). This Radical Redefinition Challenges Societal Norms And Emphasizes The Equality Of All Believers In Christ.

## *Relevance Today:*

## *1. Challenging Prejudice And Inequality:*

The Letter's Message Of Unity And Equality Speaks Directly To Modern Issues Of Discrimination, Injustice, And Marginalization. It Calls Believers To Treat Others With Dignity And Respect, Regardless Of Societal Distinctions.

- Galatians 3:28: "There Is Neither Jew Nor Gentile, Neither Slave Nor Free... For You Are All One In Christ Jesus."
- James 2:1: "Believers In Our Glorious Lord Jesus Christ Must Not Show Favoritism."

## *2. Building Inclusive Communities:*

Philemon Serves As A Reminder That The Christian Community Should Reflect The Gospel's Vision Of Inclusivity, Welcoming People From All Walks Of Life Into Fellowship.

- Colossians 3:11: "Here There Is No Gentile Or Jew, Circumcised Or Uncircumcised, Barbarian, Scythian, Slave Or Free, But Christ Is All, And Is In All."

# *The Gospel's Transformative Power*

Philemon Illustrates The Gospel's Ability To Transform Not Only Individuals But Also Social Structures. Onesimus' Transformation From A Runaway Slave To A "Useful" Brother In Christ (Philemon 1:11, 16) Demonstrates The Redemptive Power Of Faith.

## *Relevance Today:*

## *1. Individual Transformation:*

Philemon Reminds Believers That No One Is Beyond Redemption. In Christ, Lives Are Transformed, And Individuals Find New Purpose And Identity.

- 2 Corinthians 5:17: "If Anyone Is In Christ, The New Creation Has Come: The Old Has Gone, The New Is Here!"
- Romans 12:2: "Be Transformed By The Renewing Of Your Mind."

## *2. Societal Impact:*

The Letter's Implications Extend Beyond Personal Relationships To Challenge Systemic Injustices. It Encourages Believers To Reflect Gospel Values In Their Workplaces, Communities, And Society As A Whole.

- Micah 6:8: "Act Justly And Love Mercy And Walk Humbly With Your God."
- Isaiah 1:17: "Learn To Do Right; Seek Justice. Defend The Oppressed."

## *Practical Applications For Today*

The Principles In Philemon Are Not Confined To Its Historical Context. They Provide Practical Guidance For Navigating Modern Relationships, Resolving Conflicts, And Fostering Unity.

### *Examples Of Practical Applications:*

### *1. In Families:*

Philemon Teaches The Importance Of Forgiveness And Reconciliation Within Families, Helping To Restore Strained Relationships And Build Stronger Bonds.

- Proverbs 17:9: "Whoever Would Foster Love Covers Over An Offense, But Whoever Repeats The Matter Separates Close Friends."

### *2. In Communities:*

The Letter's Emphasis On Equality And Unity Challenges Communities To Create Spaces Where Everyone Feels Valued And Respected.

- Acts 2:44-47: The Early Church Modeled Fellowship And Generosity, Reflecting The Inclusivity Promoted In Philemon.

### *3. In Workplaces:*

Philemon Encourages Grace And Fairness In Leadership, Reminding Employers To Treat Employees With Kindness And

Respect.

- Ephesians 6:9: Masters Are Instructed To Treat Their Servants Well, Recognizing That Both Serve The Same Master In Heaven.

• 81 •

## *Conclusion: The Enduring Message Of Philemon*

The Book Of Philemon, Though Brief, Carries A Profound And Enduring Relevance. Its Themes Of Forgiveness, Reconciliation, And Equality Challenge Believers To Embody The Gospel In Every Aspect Of Their Lives. Paul's Appeal To Philemon Is A Timeless Reminder That The Gospel Transforms Relationships, Breaks Down Societal Barriers, And Fosters A Community United In Christ.

By Living Out These Principles, Believers Not Only Experience Personal Growth But Also Become Powerful Witnesses Of God's Love And Grace In A Divided World. The Lessons Of Philemon Remain As Relevant Today As They Were In The First Century, Offering A Roadmap For Navigating The Complexities Of Modern Life With Faith, Humility, And Grace.

# B. REFLECTING ON HOW THIS SHORT EPISTLE MODELS TRANSFORMATION THROUGH THE GOSPEL.

## _TRANSFORMATION OF INDIVIDUALS:_

## _REDEMPTION AND NEW IDENTITY_

The Story Of Onesimus, A Runaway Slave, Serves As A Striking Example Of Personal Transformation Through The Gospel. Once "Useless" In His Former Life (Philemon 1:11), Onesimus Encounters Christ Under Paul's Mentorship And Becomes A "Beloved Brother" (Philemon 1:16). The Gospel Radically Changes His Identity, Redefines His Purpose, And Restores His Worth.

- 2 Corinthians 5:17: "If Anyone Is In Christ, The New Creation Has Come: The Old Has Gone, The New Is Here!" Onesimus Is A Living Example Of This New Creation, Moving From A Fugitive To A Faithful Follower Of Christ.
- Ephesians 2:10: "For We Are God's Handiwork, Created In Christ Jesus To Do Good Works." Onesimus' Transformation Reflects His New Role As A Useful And Contributing Member Of The Body Of Christ.

Modern Application: This Message Invites Believers To See Themselves And Others Through The Lens Of Grace, Recognizing That No One Is Beyond The Redemptive Reach Of The Gospel. It Challenges Us To Embrace Our Identity In Christ, Leaving Behind Guilt And Shame, And Stepping Into The Purpose God Has For Us.

# *TRANSFORMATION OF RELATIONSHIPS:*

# *RECONCILIATION AND FORGIVENESS*

At The Heart Of Philemon Is The Reconciliation Between Philemon, The Slave Owner, And Onesimus, The Runaway. Paul's Letter Seeks To Mend Their Relationship, Urging Philemon To Forgive Onesimus And Accept Him As A Brother In Christ. This Demonstrates The Gospel's Power To Bridge Divides, Heal Wounds, And Create Unity.

- Matthew 5:23-24: Jesus Emphasizes The Urgency Of Reconciliation, Teaching That It Should Precede Even Acts Of Worship. Philemon Models This Principle As Paul Prioritizes Reconciliation Over Societal Norms.
- Colossians 3:13: "Bear With Each Other And Forgive One Another... Forgive As The Lord Forgave You." The Gospel Demands That Forgiveness Flows Freely, Just As Believers Have Been Forgiven By God.

**Modern Application:**
In Today's World, Where Divisions And Broken Relationships Are Rampant, Philemon Reminds Us Of The Importance Of Forgiveness And Reconciliation. It Challenges Us To Take Active Steps To Restore Relationships, Whether In Families, Workplaces, Or Communities, By Reflecting The Grace And Love Of Christ.

# *TRANSFORMATION OF SOCIETAL NORMS:*

## *EQUALITY IN CHRIST*

Philemon Is Quietly Revolutionary In Its Challenge To Societal Norms, Particularly The Institution Of Slavery. Paul's Appeal To Philemon To View Onesimus As More Than A Slave But As A "Beloved Brother" (Philemon 1:16) Directly Undermines The Hierarchical And Dehumanizing Structures Of The Roman Empire. While Paul Does Not Explicitly Call For The Abolition Of Slavery, His Words Sow The Seeds For Its Rejection Within Christian Ethics.

- Galatians 3:28: "There Is Neither Jew Nor Gentile, Neither Slave Nor Free, Nor Is There Male And Female, For You Are All One In Christ Jesus." This Verse Echoes The Radical Equality Proclaimed In Philemon.
- James 2:1: "Believers... Must Not Show Favoritism." Philemon Serves As A Reminder That All Distinctions, Whether Of Status, Race, Or Wealth, Are Erased In The Community Of Believers.

**Modern Application:**
The Gospel Challenges Us To Confront Systemic Injustices And Promote Equality In All Areas Of Life. Whether Addressing Racial Divides, Gender Inequality, Or Socioeconomic Disparities, Believers Are Called To Reflect The Unity And Dignity That The Gospel Brings To All People.

# *TRANSFORMATION THROUGH MEDIATION:*

## *THE MINISTRY OF RECONCILIATION*

Paul's Role As A Mediator Reflects The Intercessory Work Of Christ. Just As Paul Intercedes On Behalf Of Onesimus, Offering To Repay Any Debts (Philemon 1:18-19), Christ Stands As The Ultimate Mediator Between God And Humanity, Taking Upon Himself The Debt Of Sin To Bring Reconciliation.

- 1 Timothy 2:5: "For There Is One God And One Mediator Between God And Mankind, The Man Christ Jesus."
- 2 Corinthians 5:18-19: God Reconciled The World To Himself Through Christ And Entrusted Believers With The Ministry Of Reconciliation.

**Modern Application:**

Believers Are Called To Be Peacemakers And Mediators, Reflecting Christ's Work By Fostering Reconciliation In Their Relationships And Communities. Whether Resolving Family Conflicts Or Advocating For Peace In Divided Societies, Paul's Example Inspires Us To Actively Seek Harmony.

## *The Enduring Relevance Of Philemon*

Though Written In A Specific Historical And Cultural Context, Philemon Transcends Its Time, Offering Timeless Lessons For Modern Believers. Its Message Resonates In Personal, Relational, And Societal Contexts, Challenging Us To Live Out The Transformative Power Of The Gospel.

i. **Personal Transformation:** Philemon Reminds Us That The Gospel Renews And Restores, Calling Us To Embrace Our Identity In Christ And Encouraging Others To Do The Same.

v. **Relational Transformation:** Forgiveness And Reconciliation, Modeled In Philemon, Remain Foundational To Building Healthy, Christ-Centered Relationships.

i. **Societal Transformation:** The Epistle Challenges Societal Norms, Inspiring Believers To Work Toward Justice, Equality, And Unity, Grounded In The Gospel's Vision Of The Kingdom Of God.

## *Conclusion: A Timeless Model Of Gospel Transformation*

Philemon Is More Than A Personal Letter; It Is A Powerful Testimony To The Transformative Power Of The Gospel. It Demonstrates How The Grace Of God Can Change Hearts, Restore Relationships, And Challenge The Status Quo. Through Its Themes Of Redemption, Reconciliation, And Equality, Philemon Offers A Roadmap For Living Out The Gospel In Every Area Of Life.

Paul's Appeal On Behalf Of Onesimus Challenges Us To Reflect Christ's Love And Grace In Our Interactions With Others. It Reminds Us That The Gospel Is Not Just A Message To Be Believed But A Reality To Be Lived, Shaping Our Relationships,

Communities, And Societies. In This Way, Philemon Continues To Speak With Clarity And Conviction, Calling Believers To Embody The Transformative Power Of The Gospel In Their Daily Lives.

• 87 •

# About The Author

**Er.Venumbaka Sourab** is a passionate Teacher, Preacher, Civil Engineer, dedicated scholar, theologian, and servant of Christ with a passion for exploring the depths of Scripture and sharing its transformative truths with others, with a deep dedication to helping others understand the richness of the Scriptures. This book, **"Philemon: The Power of Love and Reconciliation," is a culmination of Sourab**'s desire to share their understanding of Paul's message with a wider audience. The Book of Philemon, often overlooked, contains urgent messages for today's believers. Holding advanced degrees in various fields and biblical studies. Sourab holds degrees a **Diploma in Education (D.El.Ed.)** from Universal Christian College Of Education, Nellore, a **Bachelor of Science (B.Sc.)** from Sri Venkateswara University, Tirupati, **Bachelor of Technology (B.Tech.)** in Civil Engineering from JNTU, Anantapur, **Master of Technology (M.Tech.)** in Structural Engineering from JNTU, Anantapur, **Master of Business Administration (MBA)** in Finance from Andhra University, Visakhapatnam, **Master of Divinity (M.Div)** from Karunya University, Coimbatore [KATE], where I delved into biblical exegesis and historical context.

- **Ministry Experience:** As a teacher & preacher, Sourab has the privilege of guiding children's ministry and youth congregations through the complexities of Scripture.
- **Research:** Sourab's research focuses on early Christian writings, and the Book of Paul has been a focal point of my scholarly pursuits.

Sourab has devoted years of study and research to understanding the intricacies of the Word of God. In this book, he unpacks its themes, explores its context, and reveals its relevance to our lives. Let's hope that readers will discover renewed faithfulness, courage, and conviction through Paul's powerful words.

With a heart for ministry and a desire to equip believers for faithful living, Sourab has served in various leadership roles within the church, including teaching, preaching, and discipleship. Through these experiences, Sourab has witnessed firsthand the profound impact that a deep understanding of Scripture can have on individuals and communities.

**"Philemon: The Power of Love and Reconciliation"** is the culmination of Sourab's lifelong dedication to studying and teaching the Word of God. Drawing on years of study, prayer, and personal reflection, Sourab offers readers a comprehensive and insightful exploration of the book of Paul, illuminating its timeless relevance for believers today.

In addition to writing and teaching, Sourab enjoys spending time with family, exploring the great outdoors, and engaging in meaningful conversations. Above all, Sourab is committed to serving the Lord with humility, integrity, and a steadfast devotion to the truth revealed in Scripture.

It is Sourab's prayer that **"Philemon: The Power of Love and Reconciliation"** will inspire and encourage readers to embrace the call to The Power of Love and Reconciliation in their own lives, as they seek to live out the timeless truths of God's Word in a world in need of hope and redemption.

Connect with **Er. V. Sourab**, Feel free to reach out to **vsourab@yahoo.com**

## *- THE END –*